P9-CRT-258

Don't Go to Work
Unless It's *Fun!*

**State-of-the-Heart
Time Management**

Don't Go to Work Unless It's Fun!

Don't Go to Work Unless It's _Fun!_

State-of-the-Heart Time Management

by

Frank Sanitate

Santa Barbara, California

Don't Go to Work Unless It's Fun!

© 1994 by Frank Sanitate Associates

All Rights Reserved. No part of the publication may be reproduced, stored in a retrieval system, or transmitted, in any form or by electronic, mechanical, photocopying, recording or other means, except for the inclusion of brief quotation on a review, without prior permission in writing from the publishers.

10   9   8   7

ISBN 1-881474-03-8
Library of Congress Catalog Card Number 94-0665-40

Santa Barbara Press • 1152 Camino Manadero, Santa Barbara, CA 93111-1063
  805-681-0589
Book design, cover design and editing by Ernest Weckbaugh,
  Casa Graphics, Inc., Burbank, CA
Manufactured in the United States of America by McNaughton
  & Gunn, Inc.

Dedication

I dedicate this book to Terry Martin Sanitate, my wife, who has always supported me in going to work and making it fun—and not going when it wasn't.

I also dedicate it to the countless workers who have had the courage to recognize when work wasn't fun, and to change the situation, or change their attitudes, or change their jobs, or change their careers.

Acknowledgments

I acknowledge and thank Fury Turner and Lorraine Cruz, two of my able assistants, for the countless hours of typing, editing and corrections they have cheerfully put into this book; Ron Hansell, Karen Cloud, and Ernie and Patty Weckbaugh for their useful editing comments and recommendations; the many participants at my workshops who have encouraged me to write this book; Barbara Gaughen for her marketing and public relations help; my children, James, Ian and Francesca, without whom this book would have come out one or two years earlier, but perhaps with less wisdom; and finally my wife, Terry, whose management of my children made it possible for the book to be published at all!

TABLE OF CONTENTS

SECTION ONE
WHY READ THIS BOOK

SECTION THREE
WORKING FOR SATISFACTION: ORGANIZATIONALLY AND PERSONALLY

SECTION FOUR
SOURCES OF DISSATISFACTION AND HOW TO GET RID OF THEM

SECTION FIVE
HOW TO CREATE SATISFACTION

Don't Go to Work Unless It's Fun!

SECTION ONE
**WHY READ
THIS BOOK?**

CHAPTER 1

WHY YOU SHOULD AND SHOULDN'T READ THIS BOOK

There are several reasons to read this book. The best one is that work can and should be fun for everyone. This book explores some of the myths that prevent work from being fun and what you can do to free yourself from these myths.

But first, let's look at some reasons why you shouldn't read this book. To say, "Don't go to work unless it's fun," shocks a lot of people. Typical responses are: "There will be a lot of people out of work." "This is impossible." "Ideally, I agree with you, but..." To them I say: Don't read this book. Some people will make the thesis of this book work for them and some won't. If you are committed to having this idea not work for you, that is, if you are going to continually try to disprove the idea that work can be fun, see if you can get a refund for the book. However, if you are committed to making your work fun, this book will help you. How do you know in which group to classify yourself? The answer is deceptively simple: Whichever group you choose to be in is the one you should be in.

In case you are still reviewing this book to try to discover the key point, here it is right now. If you find that your work is not fun for you, you have three options: change what bothers you, change your attitude or change your job. The underlying premise of these three options is: Take charge of your life; you **are** in charge. This book explores actions you can take to make work fun, but it is even more a book about attitudes. I will say little about the third option, changing jobs, but I'll give you a tip: If you are thinking right now that you probably should change jobs, you probably should!

One of my friends recently summarized my Time Management workshop as follows: Write it down, don't be a cry baby and do it! Not bad! One of the reasons people don't take charge is that they are trapped in unexamined attitudes that keep them stuck. One of the purposes of this book is to help you uncover those attitudes and to create satisfaction and pleasure in freedom of choice.

If you are committed to maximize your work life, you can. Change may not happen overnight. Tomorrow may not be an uproarious riot at work. But if you have patience and can see that you are on the road to loving your work, the process can be very satisfying—and fun.

So, if you are committed to disproving this thesis of the book, don't read it. It will do you no good. Read this book only if you are committed to making the thesis work for you.

CHAPTER 2

WHAT IS "FUN"?

In guiding you to make your work fun, I am not interested in being the Social Director on the Titanic. That is, I don't want to give you a series of tips or techniques that try to cover over fundamental problems. You may have to deal with some serious issues about your basic attitudes toward work. You may even have to quit your job! On the surface, this may not look like fun, but it is the road to creating satisfaction. A better title for this book might be, *Don't Go To Work Unless It's Satisfying.* What would it take to create satisfaction in your work and life?

Then again, dealing with a hard issue like changing jobs could be fun – if you say so. Let me give you an example. Recently while I was teaching in Vermont, 500 homes burned in Santa Barbara. Mine was in danger. My wife called me during the fire and said that she and the kids might have to evacuate. While thinking about the situation, I thought, "Here's an excellent chance to practice what I preach. How could I look at the loss of my house as an 'opportunity'? How could this be *fun?*" I actually came up with some answers. For one thing, we could rebuild our house however we wanted. We could make all the improvements we were thinking about (or *weren't* thinking about), and we'd have a brand new house. We wouldn't have to clean out the garage, or our files, or closets. We would get rid of some art which we really didn't like. We could experiment with living someplace else in town or elsewhere in the country for a while—or permanently. So, we had two options: rebuild and have fun, or rebuild and whine. Fortunately, we didn't have to choose either because the fire missed our house.

So, there are two senses of the word "fun." The first sense is: creating satisfaction. When a woman gives birth, you don't ask, "Did you have a good time?". . . and you don't have to ask, "Are you satisfied?" So, the one sense of fun is that of satisfaction, or even of joy and peace. The other sense is what most of us think of as fun: laughing and having a good time. Work ought to be that also. How often do people laugh where you work? If people are always laughing, something's wrong. If people never laugh, something's wrong. But laughter and fun have to be built on a base of satisfaction, not used to mask over dissatisfaction.

We can create satisfaction in every situation, and we can create a good time or fun in many of them.

CHAPTER 3

STATE-OF-THE-HEART TIME MANAGEMENT

What would you rather have on your tombstone: "He/she could have achieved more if he/she didn't have so much fun;" or, "He/she could have had more fun if he/she didn't achieve so much"? I am still astounded that many people pick the first. That is, they think the purpose of life is achievement, not fun.

I actually can understand how some might feel this way, because at one point in my life I too said, "Yes, I want to achieve more. Life is meant to contribute to others. The more I can do or give, the better my life will have been." This came out of a misdirected belief that it was more blessed to give, even at the expense of self-depletion. I now realize that achievement is not the purpose of life. Fun, enjoyment and satisfaction are. Achievement is the primary means of creating enjoyment, but it is the means, not the end.

In conducting time management workshops internationally since 1977, I have gradually shifted my focus from an achievement orientation to one of fun, enjoyment or satisfaction. After all, what is the appropriate amount of achievement you should have attained when you reach the grave? How often should you have achieved everything on your To Do List? How many items should you have put on each list?

I'll speak more extensively about this later. What I am getting at here is that how we spend this life is simply an extension of how we spend each day. Here is the bottom line principle to follow in life and every day: The "how much" means nothing, the "how" means everything. Not that I am against achievement. But one has to look at whether there is satisfaction in the process and satisfaction in the achievement. That is why the state-of-the-art in time management is due for a shift.

In the initial stages of time management study earlier in the century, the focus was on efficiency—how to do more in less time. Efficiency experts like Frank and Lillian Gilbreth would come into companies and do time-and-motion studies. Their purpose was to achieve greater output from the same or less input. They focused on *how* things were done.

Later in the century, Peter Drucker and others shifted the emphasis of time management from efficiency to effectiveness—working smarter. Drucker makes a nice distinction: efficiency means doing things right; effectiveness means doing the right things. Efficiency concerns itself with process—how you do things; effectiveness emphasizes end results—what you do. But both efficiency and effectiveness focus on achievement. It is time for a paradigm shift in the state of the art. *That* shift is to get in touch with our hearts concerning the use and management of time. This shift of thinking about time management is long overdue. It is a nice way to move into the next millennium.

What is "state-of-the-heart" time management? First of all, it is to start to look into your heart to understand the best use of time. What that means is to get in touch with the feelings and intuitions within. For me, this has led me to using time to achieve satisfaction and not to worry so much about achievement. In fact, the only measure of time management I use right now is my own internal state of satisfaction. And, oddly enough, I am also actually *achieving* more now! It is not the kind of achievement I would have imagined when I was focusing primarily on achievement, but it is far more rewarding. So I want to share with you some of the thoughts that have led me along this path.

State-of-the-heart time management shifts the emphasis from action to attitude. In my workshops, I originally focused on actions—what you can *do* to better manage your time. However, every action is the outgrowth of a thought, belief or attitude. Therefore, telling people how to act is useless if a negative attitude will prevent them from taking the action. So I gradually shifted to helping people reexamine and redefine attitudes as well: How do we need to look at things? What attitudes do we need to change, so that proper actions can flow automatically? This book gets beyond what we normally think of as time management—taking actions—into shifting attitudes about time, work and life.

What are the attitudes behind the practices that make people efficient, effective and satisfied? Our attitudes are the motors that drive us. If we aren't aware of them, then we are at their mercy. But if we can step back and see the attitude that creates the way we act, then we are in control. I have taught thousands of people how to manage their time more effectively. Most of the ideas I share with people have come out of looking at myself and the way I operate. I tested and continue to test their validity by sharing them and getting feedback. These ideas have been both in the realm of action and of attitude.

We are not conscious of many of our attitudes. It was surprising for me to find out in my early adulthood and after starting therapy that I was not the one who determined how I acted, but that I was at the effect of, or at the mercy of, a whole set of programmed reactions. It was only in stepping back and recognizing them that I could start to change or to accept and utilize some of them.

What is an attitude? An attitude is a combination of a thought and feeling. For example, you might have several tasks to do. The thought comes up: maybe I can't handle all of these things. The feeling comes up: I'm afraid of failing to accomplish what I should. Combined they produce the attitude of resignation. The resulting action: I'll just drift forward on this or that. But once you can identify the thought and feeling, you are in a place of freedom. You can shift your attitude by creating a new thought. In this case the thought might be: Either I will or I won't finish them all. I will work on what's important and do those things well. Your action then comes out of choice.

This book focuses on attitudes, but it will also give you practical ideas and insights. Certainly the "how to's" are valuable. They are available in much greater detail in my self-study audio-cassette program, *The New Time Management Workshop.* An order form accompanies this book. The primary purpose of this book, however, is to have you look at how you manage your time and life, to have you understand the attitudes behind your actions, and to have you get in touch with your heart. Then your primary focuswill be: what do I need to do to create satisfaction and fun in my work and in my life?

CHAPTER 4

HOW OLD DO YOU HAVE TO BE TO HAVE ENOUGH TIME ?

One of the biggest complaints I hear in the time management workshops I teach is: "I don't have enough time."

I recently gave a mini-workshop for a group of about thirty people. I was surprised to find that most of the participants were retired and probably over sixty-five. So I started the workshop by asking them to put themselves into one of three categories: I don't have enough time, I have too much time or I have just the right amount of time. To my surprise, about twenty-five of them said they didn't have enough time. One had too much time and the other four had the right amount of time. How old do you have to be to have enough time?

I am reminded of a second incident. We used to live next door to Mrs. Smith who was close to ninety years old. She lived alone and would often complain, "My upstairs is a mess. I have to get around to organizing things when I get the time." Both of these incidents make me ask, "How old does one have to be before you can say, my life is fine; my use of time is fine; things are going exactly the way they should be? When does one get rid of guilt, have exactly the right amount of time and have their life be exactly okay right now? Or, does one never reach that point?"

My answer, and the point of this book, of course, is that you *can* reach that point. Everyone can reach the point where he or she can say, "My work and my life are fine right now; they are satisfying and fun." But it will take a shift of attitude. I see clearly that no matter what age or stage in life you're at, if you don't have this attitude shift you will never be satisfied with your use of time, with your work or with your life.

CHAPTER 5

WHY DO WE WORK
SO MANY HOURS?

A few years ago, I asked a cross-section of lawyers how many worked more hours than they really wanted to. Seventy-six percent of them said they did. They worked an average of fifty-three hours per week. Overall, the hundreds of lawyers I've surveyed average fifty hours of work per week. CPAs do a little better. They average forty-seven hours per week. Of course, I have never taught CPAs during the tax season, so their hours might be considerably higher during that period of time. Why do so many Americans, especially those in these two professions, work so many hours? Is this really necessary to make a living?

I am struck by how this contrasts with some tribes described by Richard E. Leakey and Roger Lewin in their book, *People of the Lake*. They say that there are approximately 400,000 people on earth today who still make their living by hunting and gathering. In looking at how many hours these people worked each week they cite two tribes at the ends of the spectrum: "Truly objective scientific assessments of the labor of hunter/gatherers in many different environments most often come up with figures somewhere between those for the Kung [12 - 19 hours per week] and the G/wi [33 hours per week]." (Page 97) So, on the average, these most primitive tribes spend about twenty-four hours per week to make a living! My question is this, "Who is really the more primitive, these 400,000 people or us?"

There seem to be two caricatures of workers in our society. The first is of those who are overworked, stressed and who eventually burn out and have heart attacks. The second is of those with no ambition and initiative, who are doing as little as possible but just enough to avoid being fired. Both are travesties of what work fundamentally should be. It is possible for everyone to lead satisfying and productive work lives with neither overwork and stress nor loafing and boredom. This book addresses both groups of people. It also reaffirms the position of those who are in the middle—those who work happily, productively and with satisfaction.

CHAPTER 6

DON'T GO TO WORK UNLESS IT'S FUN: A NEW WORK ETHIC

We need to create a new work ethic —having work be a source of fun and satisfaction for everybody. Before looking at this new work ethic, let's look at the old one. The meaning of the old work ethic is captured in the juxtaposition of the two words, "work" and "ethic." It brings the concept of work into the realm of ethics or morality. Generally, people think of morality as a set of laws or principles to live by. To apply this to work then, if you want to be good, if you want to do the right thing, you should work. In fact, the harder you work, the better you are. This ethic doesn't stem from the principle that work is valuable, worthwhile and rewarding in itself, and therefore natural to man. It stems more from the Biblical viewpoint of Adam and Eve being cast out of the Garden of Eden with the punitive injunction, "By the sweat of your brow shall you earn your bread."

While writing this I decided to look at what the Bible actually says. I am quoting here from the *Good News Bible*, produced by the American Bible Society, Gen. 3:17-19:

> "Because of what you've done, the ground will be under a curse. You will have to work hard all of your life to make it produce enough food for you. It will produce weeds and

thorns and you will have to eat wild plants. You will have to work hard and sweat to make the soil produce anything until you go back to the soil from which you are formed."

Yikes! This is "good news"? So it's the "work is hard—life is hard—then you die" scenario which has formed the work ethic. Paradise is where no one has to work. On this earth we are all cursed to work. Nobody works because they want to; we work because we have to!

Tied in to the old work ethic is the concept that if you work hard, you will be successful. If you are successful, you will have a lot of money or property. If you have a lot of money, that is proof that you are good and that God loves you.

The work ethic, on the other hand, could be reinvented in this way. Suppose the Bible had God telling this to Adam and Eve:

"You shall have the privilege of co-creation with me. The earth is abundant and fruitful. You will be able to make and produce things, to shepherd things, to discover things that will not only help to sustain your lives but will also make your lives more enjoyable and satisfying. Discovering and producing things will give you great pleasure. You will be able to produce goods beyond your own needs and thus share goods with everyone else on the earth."

So the new work ethic is to look at work from the scenario of joy, creation, satisfaction, and fun. It is to look at work as something I want to do, not something I have to do. The thesis of this book is that work can be and *is* a source of satisfaction in our lives. If that is not true for you currently, you are not taking action on something that calls for action. Or, you have attitudes about work that are not accurate or, at least, not very useful. The purpose of this book is to share new attitudes I have discovered in consulting with others and in my journey of making my own work more satisfying to myself. Its purpose is to give you a new way to look at work and at life, so that you will naturally make those changes necessary to have your work and life become totally satisfying to you.

CHAPTER 7

WHAT PERCENT OF THE AMERICAN WORKFORCE ARE NOT SATISFIED?

I ask people at my workshops to estimate what percent of the American workforce do not get satisfaction from their work. In other words, what percent are just working to make a living and get no real satisfaction from what they are doing? The average answer I get is 66%! This is outrageous! Can this be true—two thirds of us are dissatisfied with work? It is a sad indictment for one of two reasons. First, what if the people I surveyed *are* accurate in their assessment of how many people are dissatisfied? What we end up with is one of the most productive countries on earth where the majority of people get no satisfaction from work. The second possibility is that most Americans really are satisfied with their work, but everyone walks around thinking that they aren't. That is a disempowering thought in itself. If most people are satisfied, yet we go around thinking they are dissatisfied, then we act as if it is so. If everybody acts as if it's so, it becomes a self-fulfilling prophecy. Almost everybody, in fact, does become dissatisfied.

Is work inherently dissatisfying? Is it work in America that is dissatisfying? Or is it something about the way we, as individuals, approach work that creates dissatisfaction for ourselves? Something is wrong! Read on if you want to find out what, and how to correct it.

CHAPTER 8

WHY I'M QUALIFIED TO WRITE THIS BOOK

I have always been blessed with the ability of not being able to pretend I felt good when I didn't. I've tried to pretend many times, but I always get caught in the act—especially by myself. I consider this a blessing because I have a strong suspicion that a lot of people often feel dissatisfied and disappointed, but they just cover it over, put on a happy face and keep going. On the surface this looks like a good idea. Things need to get done, tasks need to be handled, so we can't be down in the dumps. Keep your chin up and push forward. So on the surface it seems that everybody is happy. Maybe there are only a few of us who get tired, who get disappointed, who get frustrated, who get into slumps and don't want to move ahead.

I'm a little suspicious though. On the surface people look happy and yet half of our marriages break up. Were all of those couples happy up until the day they decided to get a divorce? Another example: I just mentioned that people estimate that 66% of Americans are dissatisfied in their work. Do these 66% just go around looking happy? It makes me wonder. Marriage and work are two big chunks in life that don't seem to be working out well for a lot of people. So I have to suspect that there's a lot of "positive thinking" going on—putting on a happy face that covers over a lot

of sadness, frustration, even depression. (This is a negative interpretation of "positive thinking." The rest of this book will give a
positive interpretation of it.) I haven't been able to live like that. I
know when I feel lousy.

I count this as a blessing because I haven't been willing to settle
for feeling bad and covering it up. I have always shuddered at such
stupid statements as: "Most of us live lives of quiet desperation," or,
"Life is hard, then you die." What I prefer is: "Life is hard, then you
make it easier. Then it gets a little hard again, and you make it even
easier." I don't want to gloss over being tired or glum or depressed
or incapacitated. I want to get over it. The sooner I get over it the
better. The sooner I feel better, the better. I have even gotten myself
to the point of saying, "Life is easy, and it gets easier." (Then again,
I wrote that last sentence before my third child arrived!)

Not covering things over has led me to simply admit that I am
in a lifelong quest for creating satisfaction. It has been a painfully
slow but on-going process. And it has gotten to be more and more
fun. I like the Barney's clothing store motto, "Select, Don't Settle."
My workshops and this book have developed out of this attitude.
They're for people like me who don't have it together all the time.
In fact, they're for people who want to continue to get it together,
because once you get it together you're on a new plateau. It's from
that new perspective that you can see the next thing you want to get
together. So if you're satisfied with everything in your life, don't
read this book. If you're not, read on. Take it from a pro.

CHAPTER 9

THE BASIC QUESTION

Most self-help books and tapes claim that the ideas they contain will work for you if you just put them into practice. Most of them are right. That's because most of them force you to look into yourself and draw out of yourself what is most important for your own development. Once you see, you act, and once you act, you move forward.

This book is similar. If you live in the presence of the following question, you will have everything you need to succeed in life. In fact, if you really get this question, you don't even have to read the rest of the book. Here is the question: What do I need to do to create satisfaction?

It is a deceptively simple and profound question at the same time. I am going to share with you some of the insights I have gained in my on-going pursuit of that question. Here are some I can state immediately:

- We all implicitly seek our satisfaction, but only those who explicitly seek it, find it.

- There is no one answer to the question; the answers shift and develop as our lives shift and develop.

Why Read This Book?

- Satisfaction comes only to those who create it for themselves.

- Everyone can create it.

- "You can't always get what you want. But if you try sometime, you just might find you get what you need."
  — The Rolling Stones

Whether you agree with these statements or not, the basic question of this book and of life is: What do I need to do to create satisfaction?

CHAPTER 10

SUMMARY: WHY YOU SHOULD READ THIS BOOK

In this introductory section I have talked about several ideas which have led me to write this book. There are nine reasons to read it:

1) To recognize that if you are committed to making work fun, it can be. (The opposite is equally true.)

2) To overcome the concept that work is a necessary evil.

3) To recognize that it is not external circumstances that causes work to be a source of satisfaction and fun, but it is an act of our own creation—our attitude.

4) To understand that it is our attitudes which control us, and to develop attitudes that make us not only more efficient but which will also create greater satisfaction in our work and in our lives.

5) To overcome the syndrome of, "I don't have enough time" and "I don't have enough, period."

6) To stop working such long hours, if you are doing so.

7) To overcome the perception, and possibly reality, that most of us work just to earn a living and get no satisfaction from our work.

8) To stop settling for covering up depression, anger, tiredness, glumness, but to deal with what's wrong and to keep growing.

9) To live in the basic question: What do I need to do to create satisfaction?

To accomplish these purposes, the rest of this book is divided into four main sections:

Section 2 - *Overwork: Why We Do It And How To Stop*

This section deals with one major reason work isn't fun for many people, *overwork*; and the underlying mind-set that causes it, *an attitude of scarcity*. Namely, people feel that there is not enough time, money, customers, talent, quality, life, love. This section shows how to create an attitude of adequacy and abundance to replace the scarcity mind-set.

Section 3 - *How to Create Excellence in Organizations: Working for Satisfaction*

This section shows how focusing on creating satisfaction will foster productivity, rather than vice-versa. It begins the discussion about what "satisfaction" means.

Section 4 - *Sources of Dissatisfaction and How to Get Rid of Them*

This section looks at the major external source of dissatisfaction: conflict – and the major internal ones: guilt, incompletion, indecision, lack of time control, procrastination, and being overwhelmed. It gives practical, proven ways to overcome these sources of dissatisfaction.

Section 5 - *Satisfaction and How to Create It*

This section explores the nature of work and of satisfaction. It gives seven ways to create satisfaction in work. Primary among the attitude shifts discussed is taking responsibility for your own life and moving away from victimization. It also shows how to measure your satisfaction and productivity.

CHAPTER 11

OVERWORK AND THE SEVEN SCARCITIES

The antithesis of the new work ethic – working for satisfaction and fun – is overwork. In a perverse way overworkers work to gain satisfaction. It is the satisfaction that comes from a false sense of achievement. "Look how many hours I put in; look at all the work I've done." It is false because this kind of achievement never satisfies. So before talking about creating satisfaction, I want to analyze why people overwork and what they can do to stop. But these comments aren't just for the bonafide over-worker or workaholic. They are for all of us. Everyone seems to have a fundamental attitude of scarcity lurking beneath. This is what I want to analyze and challenge.

Why do people overwork? Another way of phrasing this is: Why do we create dissatisfaction for ourselves by working longer and/or harder than we really want to? To get an insight into this, let's look at the psychology of a bully.

Why is a bully a bully? Why does he try to show his superiority or to dominate others? The answer is: He basically feels inferior to others. He feels insecure, not sure of himself. So he picks on weaker people to try to compensate for his own feelings of weakness and inadequacy. Question: How much bullying will it take before a bully realizes that he is sufficient, strong, and competent enough in himself and he doesn't need to prove himself to others? Answer: No amount of bullying will do this. Unless a bully is willing to admit his own feelings of insecurity and inadequacy, he will always be a slave to those feelings. No amount of over-compensation will get rid of those feelings. He will just start picking on bigger and bigger people or try to beat up two people at once. He will simply up the stakes in his quest to feel secure about himself. This never works. Coming to terms with his own insecurity is what it will take. (Consistently making bad judgments about whom he can bully will probably *increase* the underlying insecurity he feels!)

The reason people overwork is exactly the same. They feel insecure and inadequate, and they try to compensate for it by working too hard or too long. Yet, no matter how much they overwork, they'll never feel satisfied until they deal with the underlying insecurity. Insecurity is another way of saying: I am not adequate to handle things, or simply, I am not adequate; I don't work hard enough, long enough; I don't produce enough. I am not fast enough, smart enough, good enough.

When we apply the internal feeling of inadequacy or insecurity —of "not enough"—to the external world, we use the word, "scarcity". There's not enough time, not enough money, not enough customers. Everything is scarce. And just as the bully does, overworkers try to overcome feelings of scarcity and inadequacy by continually upping the stakes: "If I only had this much more money, if I only had this much more time, more talent, more clients, if I only work a little longer, then that will be enough!" But only when we stop over-reaching, when we come to recognize and accept the feeling of insecurity, do we begin to overcome it. Then we can stop overworking and start creating satisfaction in our lives. The feeling of "not enough" is not about external things outside of ourselves but fundamentally an internal feeling about ourselves. Recognizing and admitting this is what will allow us to move out of overworking.

So, let's explore how the feeling of scarcity or inadequacy operates in seven areas: time, money, customers/clients, talent, quality, life, and love.

CHAPTER 12

SCARCITY OF TIME:
HOW MUCH TIME IS ENOUGH?

I often ask people, "How many more hours a day would do it for you?" I get a variety of answers ranging from one or two hours, to ten or twelve, to, "I need a clone."

The reality is that we all have exactly the right amount of time right now. Twenty-four hours in a day is perfect! God spent a lot of time working out the details on this. The amount of hours we have in a day is perfect because we are the ones who choose what to do with that time. So what do we do? We over-book ourselves. What would happen if we had a twenty-eight hour day? We would then need thirty-two hours. If we had a thirty-two hour day, we'd need thirty-eight hours. We could just as easily look at it the other way. Let's pretend there were only supposed to be twenty hours in a day, and God decided to give us a bonus of four extra hours. Look how we're handling that. We've used up that bonus and are clamoring for more. And we'd continue to clamor for more with each bonus we received.

Not having enough time is just like gambling in Las Vegas. You get a thrill out of making dollar bets. But pretty soon it's not enough, so you up the stakes to two dollars. And soon that's not enough, so you up the stakes to five dollars, and to ten dollars and so on. People are always amazed at gamblers making bets worth thousands of dollars, and yet it's no different from a beginner putting a nickel in a slot machine. The high rollers simply up the stakes to the point where they get a thrill out of gambling. We do the same with time. If we gain more time, we simply up the stakes of what we want to accomplish, so that the time again becomes inadequate.

The fact about time is unchangeable: There are 24 hours in a day. However, we can interpret that fact either negatively or positively. "Not having enough time" is a negative way of interpreting it. Not having enough time really means we want to do more things than we have time to achieve. How might we reinterpret that positively? We can say: "I have more things that I want to do than I have time for. I have a multiplicity, an abundance of desires. I want the fullness of life. Life is staggeringly abundant, and I want it all! I am not narrow in my thinking and desires. My desires far outstrip the time available to achieve them. Mine is a life of abundance". We need to celebrate the fact that we want to do more than we clearly can achieve. We need to congratulate ourselves and to celebrate how big a game we're playing!

So the fact that we can't have everything we want is really good news. It means we're "big wanters." But how are we to create satisfaction in our lives when we want more than we can achieve? The answer is: to prioritize, to focus. What that means is, even though we can't have *everything* we want, we can have *anything* we want. For instance, you could become a millionaire if you wanted to. There is no question that this is possible. However, most people who say that they want to become millionaires never achieve that goal. Why? Because they are not single-minded in their purpose. They also want other things besides being a millionaire that may prevent them from becoming a millionaire. For example, to become one you might have to go back to school. You might have to go into a new career, take a second job, give up your family, give up your social life. Any of those may be required to become a millionaire. However, you say, "I want to be a millionaire, and I want to keep my family life, and I want to have leisure time, and I don't want to move from my current job or current career, etc." Too bad! There are trade-offs we must make. You can have anything you want, but you can't have everything you want.

Overwork: Why We Do It and How to Stop

Of course, you could buy a lottery ticket. But then that takes you out of the realm of controlling your life and into the realm of hope. Some people live in the realm of hope and don't even buy the lottery ticket! But if we live in the realm of controlling our life, we come down to trade-offs. We must make choices. So too with time. We have a multiplicity of desires, and we must choose among them. So now we begin to move toward the heart of satisfaction: choice.

In creating satisfaction for ourselves in the use of our time we must realize and acknowledge that we are making choices and that these choices eliminate other options. Every time we say yes to one thing we say no to everything else. We have exactly the right amount of time for the choices we are making now. We're giving up spending time on other things because of what we're choosing to spend time on now.

So there is not a scarcity of time. There's simply the reality that most of us would like to accomplish more in a given day or week or month or year or life than we have time for. Satisfaction comes from the attitude: "I have exactly the right amount of time right now. I choose to do things that are important to me. Things of lesser importance may not get done, but the important ones will. I refuse to create life-and-death situations out of those things that don't get done. In fact, I am proud that there are things that don't get done because it means that I have a fertile mind and imagination. I am always creating many new possibilities for myself. I clearly know I can't achieve all of them but I am pleased to have such a large menu to choose from." In short, there is not a scarcity of time; there is simply an abundance of desires on my part.

CHAPTER 13

SCARCITY OF MONEY:
HOW MUCH MONEY IS ENOUGH?

People do not really overwork because they want to make more money. Making more money will never ultimately satisfy us. Money is just like time: The more we have, the more we want. I remember talking to my friend, Marty, when we were driving up to the country one weekend. We were talking about money and hunger in the world. At the end of our conversation, he agreed that once he had a million dollars he would give away everything else that he made. At the end of the weekend, he came up to me and said, "I've been thinking it over; let's make it two million." His needs jumped from one to two million over the weekend!

Similarly, in the late 70's, my wife and I said that once we made $30,000 a year we would be satisfied. That would be enough income to take care of our needs and we'd give everything else away. We hit that level the following year and found to our surprise that it was clearly not enough money. So we upped the stakes. Now, that amount can't even pay our mortgage.

The best explanation of why we keep upping the stakes is Abraham Maslow's "Hierarchy of Needs." We all have a variety of needs, some lower level and some higher level. Once we achieve the lower level needs we are not satisfied. We move to the higher level needs. We are never satisfied when we reach our goal because we always create a higher one. Let's explore these needs.

On the lowest level we have to satisfy our physiological needs: food, shelter, clothing, etc. When we have enough money to do this, we are not satisfied. We want more and better food, better clothing, better housing. But once our physiological needs are relatively taken care of, are we satisfied? No, Maslow says. We then become concerned about our security needs. Security means physical safety for one thing, freedom from threat. But it also means psychological safety as well. We can provide our food for today, but will we have enough tomorrow? Security is the next level up in the hierarchy. So we start accumulating money so that we can have enough to cover our basic needs for a week or a month or a year. But how much is enough?

I remember speaking with two of my co-workers in 1970. We were talking about how much money you should have in the bank to be secure. I said $1,000. My friend said, "That's ridiculous. You need at least $2,000." My other friend laughed at both of us, but he refused to give a figure. He already was on the security bandwagon. He had accumulated $1,000, but knew it wasn't enough, and then $2,000, but knew it wasn't enough and so on. So what happens is that your perception of your needs increases based on where you are now. The more you have now, the more you "need." So what you need for security is relative.

Maslow says that once your security needs are satisfied, you become concerned about your social needs—the need to be loved and to love. And from there you go on to the need for esteem. People also use money in these two areas. They try to buy affection and buy esteem: If you have a lot of money people will like you and they will respect you. After a certain level of income, business executives do not want raises because they're hungry or they need to save for a rainy day. A pay increase becomes a measure of how much they are esteemed and valued by their companies or society. Yet, if you don't have self-love or self-esteem, no amount of money can ever buy them.

The highest level in Maslow's hierarchy of needs is self-actualization. This means to achieve your full potential, to make a unique contribution, to do what you do as an expression of who you are. Money actually can be used appropriately at this level. Philanthropists use money to fulfill their desire to make a better world. Their lives are about improving the world. Some people use money to try to buy self-actualization. They play bigger and bigger games with money simply because they like to play games. They will accumulate enough stock so that they can eventually control a company. They will jump from the $100,000 real estate deal to the million dollar deal. Just as in Las Vegas, they get their thrills by upping the stakes. But the difference with self-actualizing people is that they know that accumulation doesn't satisfy. They know this is a game, and they play because they love to play. So there can never really be enough money at this level because there is always a bigger game to create.

In short, if we try to use money to buy satisfaction it won't work; there will never be enough because we always up the stakes. On the level of physical need we always want bigger and better material goods. We always want more and more security, a bigger and bigger cushion—if not for us, then for our descendants. We always want more affection and esteem.

How does one get out of the accumulation trap? Once we realize that there is never enough money in the accumulation game, we are free to reverse the statement. We can change our attitude from a negative one of scarcity to a positive one of abundance. We can say: I have precisely the right amount of money now; I have exactly enough.

Having enough doesn't preclude wanting more, it just means: "I am satisfied now and wouldn't mind having more. I don't need more and, if by some twist of fate this level of income is all that I would have, it would be adequate." It is only when you make this basic shift in attitude that you can create satisfaction in your life about money. If you still have the urge to try to use money to buy security and esteem, then talk to a therapist. You need to get in touch with your basic feelings of insecurity and inadequacy, reexperience where they came from and complete them.

So people don't overwork for money. Healthy individuals may work overtime temporarily to earn extra money, but then they go back to their normal income level. But for workaholics it becomes a habit. You justify the overwork by saying it's for the money. But if you feel inadequate within, money is just like time: There is never enough. And the same attitude shift needs to take place with money as with time: I have a multiplicity of desires for which I need money. Since I can't have them all right now, I declare that I have exactly the right amount of money for my needs now.

CHAPTER 14

SCARCITY OF CUSTOMERS/CLIENTS/JOBS: HOW MANY ARE ENOUGH?

Another reason people give for overworking is that there is a scarcity of customers or clients or jobs.

Let's begin with those who sell professional services to clients. One lawyer said to me, "I specialize in what comes in the door." Many professionals have that attitude; it's the attitude of survival. We have to take every client who comes in the door. It's probably an appropriate attitude when you first start your business. You are concerned about survival and so whatever business there is, you take it. But some firms are still in a survival mode after five or ten or fifty years of operating. They never say "no" to a client; they never turn anyone away. There is a nagging fear in the back of their heads: "If I turn one client away, all of them will leave. And no more will come." The reality is that there are plenty of clients, there is plenty of work.

If you do your best job there will always be plenty of clients. Why do clients and customers come to you in the first place? You're fulfilling a need that they have. I often ask people in my workshops: When is the last time you had too little work to do? Many people are overworked, and yet, they worry about turning away business. Work on the clients who count, the customers who count, the areas that count and don't worry about the ones you don't service.

Overwork: Why We Do It and How to Stop

Another way of saying this is: Specialize. And along with special-ization, consider raising your fees or prices.

Related to this is a question I often ask my clients, "Which would you rather do, double your present income and work the same amount of time, or keep your present income and work half the time?" About two thirds of them want to double their income and one third want to cut their time in half. Fortunately, the same method can be used to achieve either goal. That is: Simply double the fees that you charge clients. If you lost half of your clients, you'd still be making the same amount of money. Then you can use the time to play golf! Or if you're interested in the money, use the time to go out and develop more clients who can pay the fees that you require!

Doubling your fees is generally not literally feasible. However, one CPA told me that he did almost that. He raised his fees 85% over a three-year period. He told all of his clients that he was going to do this and kept track of how many he lost. He lost only 11% of his clients. A variation on the theme: If you want to work 10% less, charge your clients 10% more and fire 10% of your clients.

The unfortunate thing is that many professionals do raise their fees but they don't stop overworking. They simply make more money and still overwork. Why is this so? The answer is that either they don't like their life outside of work or they have insecurity at a deeper level, which I will discuss as we move on.

To further refine this concept: Are there *really* enough clients? Are there really enough customers? Is there really enough work for everyone? If you're in the buggywhip business you have a prob-lem. People just don't buy buggywhips like they used to, or daisywheel printers, or American cars for that matter. However, if we look at what the customer wants, there is still plenty of work to do. People do not buy your products or services because they wish to give you a comfortable life. They buy them to fulfill *their* needs. If your products don't fulfill their needs, people stop buying them. If you stop focusing on selling what you have to sell and look at what people want to buy, you will never run out of work. In reality, sometimes what we have been doing does become inadequate to the needs of the marketplace. So the focus of our efforts needs to be not in creating new buggywhip promotions but in developing our businesses in areas that will fulfill the needs of our customers. Maybe the smart buggywhip makers became the suppliers of upholstery for automobiles. As long as you focus on fulfilling a need, there are always plenty of customers, clients and work.

Let me digress on the question of "creating jobs." The reality is that we don't need to create jobs; there are plenty of jobs around. But to understand this we have to look at what a job is. A job is doing something to provide goods or services that fulfill a particular need. So the source of jobs is needs. If you look around America as I am writing this today, there are a multitude of needs. There are millions of homeless. There are millions of drug addicts. There are needs for low-cost homes, for job training, for social skills training, for psychotherapy, for medical attention, for childcare, even for English language training. So there is not a scarcity of jobs; jobs are abundant. What our government needs to ask, if it wants to create jobs in America, is, "What are our needs, and how can we use our resources to fulfill these needs?"

"That's great on a global or national perspective," you say, "but what about me as an individual looking for a job right now?" I still say there is a job for everybody. If you are committed to looking at needs and how your talents can fulfill those needs, you can find or create a job. However, if you choose to make getting a new job your primary focus, you may have to give up some other things. You may have to retrain. You may have to move to another state. You may have to change careers. Remember, you can't have *everything* you want, but you can have *anything* you want.

So there really is not a scarcity of clients, customers, work or jobs. We don't need to overwork by taking in every client or by working so hard at this job because there are no other jobs available. To get over the attitude of scarcity about jobs, we need to make the same affirmations as with money and time: There is an abundance of clients, customers and jobs, and I have the capacity of generating more.

CHAPTER 15

SCARCITY OF TALENT:
HOW MUCH TALENT IS ENOUGH?

Now we shift to a deeper level of scarcity. The first three types of scarcity are those we attribute to external things: Time, money, customers/clients/jobs. Now we come to internal scarcity, a feeling of inadequacy about oneself. This feeling can exist at several levels. The first is the feeling of scarcity or inadequacy concerning our talent. Talent might be defined as intelligence, skill and motivation. Some people overwork because they feel they lack talent, they're "not good enough." But that feeling is generally inaccurate. This applies to both employers and employees.

If you are an employer or an entrepreneur, you run your own business. Whether you provide services or goods, you clearly had the brains and the talent to get you where you are now. The next challenge may be how to switch from buggy whips to upholstery. In other words, if you see the need for what you produce dropping off, your challenge is to focus more on what customers need rather than on what you produce. Failure to do this means allowing your unexamined feeling of inadequacy to overcome what you have already accomplished. Your creativity and talent got you to where you are. It will take you to where you're going.

If you are an employee, inadequacy shows up as, "I am afraid to make requests or demands here, and I am afraid I can't get another job." People don't actually come out and say this—it would be healthy if they did—but it is a prevalent attitude. If you have a boss who doesn't support your best interests or desires, when do you start saying "no" to him or her? How long, in reality, would it take you to find another job? The only thing that prevents us from asking for what we want, either in this job or in finding the next, is the sense of inadequacy, of scarcity of talent.

If you are one of the people I'm describing, look at it this way: You've fooled people all along the line to get where you are, and you're fooling your present boss right up to today. This is obviously true since you haven't been fired yet. So why don't you just fool someone on the next level up, that is, in your next job? The only reason you've arrived at where you are right now is that you had the talent to grow into that job. That same talent can take you to your next level.

Another possibility is that you are in a job right now that actually is too big for you. It's too demanding because you have bitten off more than you can chew. Or your boss is over-demanding. There are two possibilities in this situation: you may be growing into the job, or you may be in over your head. If you have the sense that you are growing into the job, great. If not, clearly you should get your responsibilities reduced or leave the job. If the job is too big, if you really *are* inadequate to handle it, get rehired down to the level where you can meet the demands. Why torture yourself just for money?

In reality though, most of us really are adequate to the job we're doing. Not that there aren't challenges or that there isn't room for growth. It's just the undiscovered or unspoken feeling of inadequacy or scarcity of talent that makes us overcompensate by overworking. All that we really need to do is to declare that our talents have been enough to get us this far, and they will take us to the next level.

CHAPTER 16

SCARCITY OF QUALITY: HOW GOOD IS GOOD ENOUGH?

Tied in with the scarcity of talent is the scarcity of quality. That is, people aren't sure of the quality of the work they do: Is the work I do good enough? They feel it isn't, so they overcompensate by putting in quantity; that is, they work longer hours. This is a trap because what they are really doing in putting in 50% of their time perfecting the last 10% of the job. If we come from an attitude of inadequacy, then we will always feel inadequate about the quality of our results. The inadequacy comes from our own feelings rather than the results themselves. It's not so much that the _work_ isn't good enough; it's _I'm_ not good enough.

The reality is that in any job you can always put in more time and add to the quality. For example, in a written report, you can always come back for a third, fourth and fifth edit and find some things to improve. However, we reach the point of diminishing returns. We're getting less and less marginal return for more and more effort. Ultimately we may sabotage ourselves by not getting it out to our audience in time to do any good. If we had an infinite amount of time to work on each thing, then we could perfect each thing we do. However, in the real world, doing your best always means doing your best in the time you allot to a given project. Clearly we ought to allot more time to important activities and to limit the time we spend on less important ones. If it's important, we should take whatever time it requires. But we need to give up the idea of being a perfectionist in *everything*.

There are two ways to choose a stopping point for a task. One is to say: "I've given as much time to this task as I'm going to. I choose to stop here. This is the best I can do in this amount of time." The second way is to work until some external event gives us an excuse to stop. For example: "I've worked two hours overtime and I must get home to my family;" or, "I'm starving and I must get something to eat because I can't think clearly;" or, "It's almost midnight and I must get some sleep;" or, "Another client is screaming on the phone and I must handle that." All of these latter choices put us at the effect of circumstances. We let circumstances make decisions for us, rather than deciding for ourselves. I suggest the former method for stopping a task. A friend adopted the philosophy: "Good enough is good enough."

I ask lawyers, "When are you adequately prepared for trial?" The correct answer is, "When it's over." There is always more you can do to prepare. Similarly, a CPA told me, "You audit until the train leaves." That is, there's always more you can do, more you can look for. Perhaps it's fear of the client's accusation, "You could have done better." More often than not, it is our *self*-accusation that drives us.

To achieve overall quality in our lives then, we must give up quality on individual items. We must be able to say to ourselves: "I am producing overall quality results. I am committed to many things; I complete what's important with quality, and I live with imperfection in minor things." So quality really comes down to declaring that what we do is good enough. We must simply say: "I am adequate. I have done an adequate job. I have done the best I can. I have done my best, not because some external circumstance stopped me, but because I decided to stop. I say this is enough, and that the marginal return on any further effort is not going to be worth it. Good enough is good enough!"

I know this may fly in the face of current slogans like, "good enough isn't!" But the push for total quality in business may destroy the quality of the lives of workers. I am not in favor of producing shoddy quality, but as individuals and as a society we need to challenge the false assumptions, "more is better" and "better is better." You can always do more, you can always do better, but at what price? We must strive for the highest quality in our life, and work is just part of life—not vice-versa.

On another level, however, there is yet a better way to achieve overall quality in your work. That is, focus more and more on things that count and just stop doing things that don't count. Then we can move toward the state: I only do what counts, and I give each thing the time it needs. So we give up trying to do everything, and do a top quality job on everything we do undertake. As people mature, they operate more and more in this fashion. However, if you are a perfectionist who is never satisfied, then even if you undertake only *one* thing in life it won't be good enough. What you do will be good enough in quality only when you are able to say, "*I* am good enough." Scarcity of quality is overcome by affirming your own quality.

CHAPTER 17

SCARCITY OF LIFE: HOW MUCH LIFE IS ENOUGH?

Perhaps all of the previous scarcities boil down to the one fundamental scarcity: The scarcity of life. That is, we feel that our life isn't good enough, full enough, long enough. In short, we are afraid of death.

Nobody wants to die. We have the demand: I want *more* life; I want *fuller* life. So we live in a constant state of scarcity with regard to life itself. I ask the question in my seminars: "How many have the sense that if you were to die today your life would be complete? Not that there's not more you want out of life, but you could declare it to be complete now?" Very few say they can. Yet, if your life is not complete now, if your life is "not enough" now, when will it ever be complete? Is it when that last, final, external circumstance —death—moves in and tells you, "Your life is now complete"? It was incomplete a minute ago, but now all of a sudden it's complete. Many people don't get to, or choose to, "complete" their life even at the point when they actually die. Even in old age many simply pass from desires to regrets. They pass from "it ought to be more" to "it should have been more."

What does it mean to have your life be complete right now? It means nothing is lacking. However, most people live in scarcity, the feeling that there isn't enough: I don't have enough, I don't do enough, I am not enough, I am inadequate, I am not worthwhile. This is a lack of self-worth or self-esteem. However, if I have self-esteem, if I declare my own worthwhileness, nothing is lacking in me or the external world. What I have right now is enough. What I have achieved up to this point is enough. What I am is enough. Not that I don't want more, want to do more, want to live more and be more—that would be fine. But nothing is lacking right now. So, I am free to die at any moment. My life is complete at any moment.

To be able to make the affirmation, my life is complete right now, you would have to declare, "*I* am complete right now." So, not enough "life" boils down to not enough "me." It means *I* am lacking, *I* am inadequate, *I* don't have self-worth. This leads us to a fundamental question: where does the attitude of self-worth or self-esteem come from?

CHAPTER 18

HAVE–DO–AM

People generally try to overcome the scarcity they feel about themselves, their feeling of lack of self-worth, in three ways. They try to derive self-worth from:

1) What I have,
2) What I do, or,
3) What I am.

The first way people try to overcome scarcity is to focus on "having," to continually strive to have more things—to accumulate. I love the irony of the saying: "He who has the most toys when he dies, wins". You end up with neither the toys, nor the prize, nor the win. Somehow the game of accumulation puts off facing the reality that some day I won't be here. If I stop accumulating, the next question I would have to ask is, "What shall I do with my life?" Since people often are afraid to look at the answer, they put off the question by continuing to accumulate: "My life must be worthwhile, because of all that I have!" So it is the underlying sense of inadequacy that makes us accumulate. Yet, as I discussed earlier, we can never accumulate enough to make us feel adequate. Adequacy or self-worth doesn't come from what we *have*.

The second way people try to overcome the sense of scarcity or lack of self-worth is: I am worthwhile because of what I *do*. This is what makes overachievers overachieve: "My life will be worthwhile if I can reach this income level, if I can bring is these new accounts, if I can produce this new product, if I can sell to this many customers, if I can get these ten things done by the end of the day, etc." There is a need to achieve, the need to set goals and accomplish them. This can be a source of great satisfaction in life, but it is not *the* source of satisfaction. Doing is not what ultimately makes us adequate and worthwhile.

It's easy to see this when we compare trying to create adequacy out of *doing* with trying to create it out of *having*: "He who has the most toys when he dies wins," equates to "he who accomplishes the most by the time he dies wins." Accomplishment is also a never-ending game where we continue to up the stakes. If we bring in ten new clients, we go for twenty; if we bring in twenty, we go for forty. If we've developed one new product we start to develop a second. If we've built ten buildings, we go for fifteen. If we complete twenty phone calls in one day we go for thirty. And so on.

So the process of accomplishment, doing, is the same as the process of accumulating. If we pin our hopes on creating self-worth and satisfaction out of them, we get trapped in the ever-ascending spiral of upping the stakes. Many of us are so bent on the pursuit of accomplishment that it's like a headlong dash to the grave. When we reach the grave we say, "I finally made it!" That means we've missed the whole point. The point is, that it's not so much the getting *there* (accomplishing goals) that counts, but the *getting* there (enjoying the process).

If we don't get a sense of adequacy or worth from having and doing, where does it come from? The answer is: from being. I am worthwhile, not because of what I have or what I do, but simply because I *am*. I don't have to have anything, I don't have to do anything, and, in fact, I don't even have to be anything specific to be worthwhile. My very being constitutes my worth. The fact that I am, that I exist, makes me worthwhile. But what is the reason for our worthwhileness? The answer is that there is no reason. We are worthwhile simply because we exist, with nothing added. It is true that we exist *as* havers and doers. We do spend most of our time on the planet accumulating and producing. But these are not the source of our adequacy or worthwhileness—our being is.

Don't Go to Work Unless It's Fun!

From a spiritual point of view, God made the universe and it is good. I am part of that universe. I am here. He/she (I'll say "he" from now on for simplicity's sake) must have made me. I am automatically good, worthwhile, adequate, simply because I'm here. God doesn't have a target for what he wants us to accumulate or accomplish. Even if he did and we blew it, he's probably big enough to make things work out in the long run. (He's probably even big enough to handle my using small "h's.") After all, it's his show, not ours. If you don't believe in God, then the universe is running the show, and it put you here as one of the players. You *must* be OK.

So, if we are automatically adequate and worthwhile, how do we handle it when we don't *feel* so? At one level we feel inadequate when we fail in our having or our doing—we don't meet our expectations, we don't get or achieve something we wanted. At this moment we have the option to say either, "Things didn't turn out as I expected, and I am inadequate," or, "Things didn't turn out as I expected, and I am adequate." The choice is to have our feeling dictate our self-worth or for *us* to dictate our self-worth. Ultimately everything is worthwhile whether it feels so or not, whether it says so or not. Even the person who commits suicide is worthwhile—but it would have made a big difference if he had affirmed it to himself!

How does one establish a sense of adequacy? It comes solely from our affirmation that we are worthwhile, and it's an affirmation that only we can make. No one else can make it for us. It is the essence of what it means to be human: simply to affirm that we exist and we are worthwhile. Everything else in the universe exists. Man is the only being who knows he exists. Therefore, he is the only being that can affirm his existence. On the other hand, he can also negate it. This is the awesome power of what it means to be human. You get to decide whether you are worthwhile or not, and it is for no other reason than you say so. The universe, of course, already decided you are worthwhile, but you still get to decide one way or the other for yourself.

When you make this fundamental decision about your own worth, everything else falls into perspective. The proper attitude then becomes: "Sometimes I'm a rock and sometimes I'm a rocket."

Overwork: Why We Do It and How to Stop

We have the seasons of our life, and even seasons of our day. Sometimes we are quite productive and fruitful and other times we are not. Our value doesn't come from that but from our own being.

This declaration about our worthiness comes out of humility rather than pride. As if we had very much to do about our being here in the first place, about the genes we possess, about the talent we possess, about the circumstances that surround us and the opportunities that offer themselves to us. We think that when we are accumulating or producing we are *doing* something. The reality is that we are not doing anything, we are *accepting* something. When we strike oil we don't create the oil, we just accept it. When we discover berries, or harvest a field, or take advantage of an opportunity, or even have a thought, we are not doing; we are receiving, accepting. So our job in life is to simply look for things to accept —and accept them. When we receive them, we accept a new gift. If we don't receive them, we can be happy with the gifts we already have. Our very being is a gift we had nothing to do with producing. Our only job is to affirm it: "I saw the world, including me, and it was good."

If we look at this idea from a biblical context, the story of Job comes to mind. He had many gifts from God and was grateful. He lost them all and was still grateful. "The Lord giveth and the Lord taketh away; blessed be the name of the Lord." He recognizes that he didn't have a right to any of it in the first place and it was all a gift from God. He still had the gift of life and was open for whatever came next for him.

Another way of looking at it is: God doesn't make junk. When you're a rock that's okay with him. When you're a rocket that's okay, too. God doesn't care what level you're operating at in the universe today. "I'm not a cellist today, I'm not the President today; maybe tomorrow, maybe not." God won't be disappointed.

So, self-acceptance doesn't depend on our reaching our goals, fulfilling our expectations. Disappointment comes from not getting what we want - unfulfilled expectations. Two ways to prevent yourself from being disappointed are:

1. Don't want or expect anything.

2. Want or expect anything you like and work for it, but don't link your sense of worth to whether you achieve it or not: "I had hoped to be a rocket today, but I am a rock. Blessed be the name of the Lord."

God doesn't cheer when something happens. "Hey, this rock shifted an inch today; hey, this person became President today; hey, another supernova blew out today." The universe is an ongoing process. As little "creators" we make plans about the pace and direction humanity moves in. When things don't go as we planned, the proper attitude is, "Okay, okay, I was just pretending that I was running the show. I am pleased to step back and see how the show really is running. I am pleased to be part of it in the first place."

If you think that there is an answer "out there" to the question, "Who am I?" then you are still trapped in trying to create meaning out of what you have or do. The answer to the question, "Who am I?" is: whomever I am creating myself to be at this moment. This frees us to constantly recreate who we are. This is the opportunity and the meaning of what it is to be human. It's not only to exist but to have the opportunity to continually create our existence at each moment. What we create is not what's significant. What is significant is the process of creation, of being.

So the sixth scarcity is a feeling of inadequacy about our lives. "My life is not adequate, not long enough, not good enough" equates to, "*I* am not adequate." Just as with not having enough or not doing enough, so too we can have the feeling of not *being* enough. They are all overcome by the affirmation: I have enough, I do enough, I am enough. My life is complete at this moment!

CHAPTER 19

SCARCITY OF LOVE:
HOW MUCH LOVE IS ENOUGH?

It wasn't until the third editing of this book that it occurred to me I was missing the most fundamental scarcity which causes overwork. And that is the scarcity of love. Perhaps it eluded me because it is so obvious and so fundamental. Why do people spend so much time trying to prove themselves, especially through overwork? The answer is simple: We need the approval of other people. We need other people to see what we do and say how good we are. We need them to say that they respect us, they like us, they love us.

In the last chapter, I talked about the scarcity of life, the feeling that we are not worthwhile just as we are. Why wouldn't people feel adequate or worthwhile just the way they are? The answer is that they weren't affirmed enough as children, they weren't accepted enough, they weren't told and shown enough that they were okay just the way they were. Earlier, I asked, why does the bully bully? The answer is because he feels insecure. Why does he feel insecure? It's because he wasn't affirmed enough or loved enough as a child. So the roots of insecurity for all of us go back to a scarcity of love in our childhood. That scarcity may be true or imagined, but it is there and real for many people.

Before I went in to therapy and before I had children, I used to think that if a child felt he wasn't loved enough, it was totally the parents' fault. But as I grow older and watch my children grow, I think that perhaps the feeling of not enough love may even be genetic for some people! I suspect that most, if not all, of us felt a scarcity of love and approval in our childhood and that it is not our parents' fault, but it is in the nature of things. It's just the way things are. Perhaps this is what the philosophers meant by "lacrimae rerum"—"the tears of things," "the tears of the universe." The fact is that children *are* inadequate to live in the adult world. That's what constitutes them as children. So many of our conversations with them are in the nature of, "Don't pick up your spaghetti with your fingers, don't spill your milk, did you finish your homework, don't mumble, your room is only half clean, etc." I am often on my children's case, just as my parents were on my case. It's an expression of love which doesn't look like an expression of love (or, is it an expression of my neuroses!). The bottom line is that our parents loved us the best they could.

Now "the best they could" is, in reality, not good enough in some cases. Parents who abuse or molest their children love them as well as they can, but it's not good enough. In nine cases out of ten they themselves were abused or molested, and they have never been able to free themselves from that trauma and are thus trapped into repeating the behavior. Even in the case of a "normal" parent, such as myself, I find that my love is sometimes good-willed but badly executed. For example, when I correct my nine-year-old for six different things in a row, I am sometimes able to pull back and say, "What's happening with *me* that my entire conversation is one negative thing after the other?" I also give my children a lot of kissing and hugging and positive statements as well, but who knows how they will look upon me when they grow up.

I say this because I used to put a lot of blame on my parents. I should more rightly have put it on the nature of things. For example, I was one of seven children, and I didn't feel that my mother loved me. I actually remember one incident where I pretty much decided that she didn't love me. It was when I woke up from having my tonsils out and having a terrible dream while I was under ether. When I looked at her she had a stern look on her face, but I wanted her to smile. Since she wasn't smiling at that point, I concluded that she didn't love me. Never mind that she was probably anxious or concerned about me; never mind that she had other concerns as well. She didn't follow the rules that I set up in my head, and so I concluded that she didn't love me. As an adult, I came to recognize how silly that decision was, but it governed a lot of my life for forty years. I also concluded that, since I only had one seventh of her time, I didn't have one hundred percent of her love. Perhaps life would have been better for me if I were an only child or had only one sibling. But then again, I would have missed out on some great siblings and a myriad of wonderful nieces and nephews. Maybe it would have been better, but that's not the way it was, and is. I now realize that given the way it was and is, my mother loved one hundred percent.

My children will grow up making whatever conclusions they make. I hope they realize the love their parents have for them. Maybe I'll just show them this chapter of the book when they're twenty-one or so!

If you feel that your parents didn't love you, or you feel that you don't have enough love in your life right now, or you feel that you are driven to achievement and driven to overwork and you can't seem to get out of it—what should you do? The thing to do is get help. Generally, the best place to get help is from a professional. If you have appendicitis you don't go to a dentist. So if you have emotional problems, with behaviors you can't seem to change, you go to a psychotherapist. They may cost a lot of money, but if you have appendicitis you don't quibble over the cost.

You don't necessarily have to go into therapy. You may have a minister or a good friend to talk to, or you may go to self-help seminars or twelve-step programs that can help you understand and handle addictive behavior. I spent several years in therapy at one point in my life and several sessions at another point. Both have proven immensely valuable to me in helping me to recognize some of the addictive behaviors in my life, to recognize where they came from, to re-experience some of those previously hidden incidents in my life and to move forward with greater freedom. I recommend it for anyone.

The value of working with a therapist is that it is an ongoing relationship. It requires commitment. A professional can help you confront yourself. Since you pay for it, you take it seriously. So if you recognize a scarcity of love in your life, my main suggestion is to get some help, and the primary means of getting help is therapy. In addition, I suggest the following affirmation: "I am totally loved and totally loving." If regular use of this affirmation doesn't create the feeling of being loved, the feeling of adequacy, then a therapist is in order.

How much love is enough? Just as with the other six scarcities you have exactly the right amount of love right now. You received one hundred percent of what your parents could give and you have one hundred percent of the love of the universe available to you now. The only limit to what you can receive is your willingness to drop the barriers that prevent you from receiving more.

SUMMARY — THE SEVEN SCARCITIES

In summary, we have reviewed the seven scarcities and how they affect our lives. They are not only the source of overwork, but the source of dissatisfaction in our lives. Since these scarcities aren't factual but are interpretations of facts, the way to overcome them is to re-interpret the facts. I hope you can use these insights to create a sense of abundance in the universe and a recognition of your adequacy and worth as an individual. If you overwork, I have suggested getting help. I also suggested creating affirmations that restructure how you look at reality.

In the next chapter I will give you some further insights into the process of creating affirmations and summarize some affirmations that will help you overcome workaholism and a sense of scarcity or inadequacy. Then I will suggest an action you can take to meet workaholism or overwork head-on and deal with it.

CHAPTER 20

HOW TO CREATE ADEQUACY: AFFIRMATIONS

How does one change a fundamental way of looking at life, an ingrained attitude? Specifically, how can you create a sense of adequacy in yourself when you feel inadequate? Simply put, the answer is: recognize the attitude, acknowledge that you are creating it, and create a different attitude. The way to do this is to use positive affirmations about yourself.

An affirmation is a statement that affirms what's so. The power of an affirmation is that it actually creates what's so. But let's make a distinction. Affirming that you are six feet tall won't make a bit of difference if you are five feet eight. Affirmations are not meant to cover up the truth. But what is "truth"? Truth can mean basic facts, and it can mean how you *interpret* the facts. Affirmations apply to how you interpret the facts, not to the facts. If you are five feet eight you can affirm, "I am too short," or you can affirm, "I am the perfect height." In either case, your affirmation is what creates the reality.

Another example: Let's say the fact (what happened) is that you were fired from your job. How do you interpret that fact? You can call yourself a failure or you can call yourself a success. It is only saying "I am a failure" that makes you such. Saying "I am a success" makes you a success. It is what you say that creates the reality. Even though something may not have been so in the past, we can create it to be so in the future simply by our statement. Again, I am speaking here about changing our attitudes, not about changing specific facts. Another example: You have $10,000 in the bank. You can interpret that fact in two ways: either, "I don't have enough money," or "I do have enough money." The fact—the amount of money you have—doesn't change, but the reality you make of it is what you create by your saying so, by what you affirm. So if you have been affirming scarcity in the past, you can supplant that by affirming adequacy or even abundance now.

Let's look at two types of affirmation. The first type is one you make about yourself. It starts with "I am." Some examples would be: "I am a loving father and husband," "I am a successful business person and feel good about my accomplishments," "I am an honest person," "I am a hard worker who is successful," "I am a caring and good person," "I am energetic," "I am a responsible and dependable worker," "I am a sympathetic person who cares about other people and their feelings." All of these are true simply because you made it up, you said so. The power of affirmations is that they are acts of creation: you become what you affirm.

To be powerful, an affirmation should not say, "I would like to be," or "I strive to be," or "I hope to be," but "I am." It also should not contain a negative. "I am not miserly" still fixes our attention on the idea of miserliness. A workable affirmation would be, "I am generous," or "I grow more generous every day." At any moment you can be what you say simply because you say so. It is the affirmation that starts to transform us. Negative thoughts or negative attitudes, even if we have carried them with us for a long time, lose their power if we supplant them with a positive affirmation. I suggest that you create one or two special affirmations about yourself which empower you, write them down and say them each day.

A second type of affirmation is not about yourself but about how you relate to the world. One of my favorite affirmations which has helped shift my attitude from one of scarcity to one of abundance is: "I have all the time in the world. I have all the energy in the world. I have all the resources in the world. I have all the love in the world." This is an affirmation of what is so, not what I hope will be so. I *do* have all the time in the world. Twenty-four hours are allotted every day to each individual and I have all of those twenty-four hours to use as I please. The way I am structured and the way the world is structured is that energy flows from the world through me and back into the world. I have the total allotment of energy that comes to me at my disposal. Similarly, I have all the resources in the world. Whatever I open myself up to in the world I can receive and use. And I have all the love in the world. That is, I am able not only to receive the resources, but I put them back into the world. I am in communion with the universe. This second type of affirmation shifts the way you look at external reality by actually creating the reality. It is not make-believe; it is a fundamental statement about the way things are which you create, which makes sense to you, and which gives you power.

To further clarify how affirmations work, let's look at the distinction of "living into" and "living out of." An affirmation is something you live into at first, and it eventually becomes something you live out of. Take for example the affirmation I used in the last paragraph: "I have all the time in the world." When I first started to use that affirmation it certainly didn't *feel* like I had all the time in the world. But I also knew that it was a more empowering way of interpreting 24 hours than, "I don't have enough time." So, I was "living into," growing into, the affirmation. Gradually, by continually affirming that I had enough time, I naturally started to shift my behavior so that I experienced more and more that I *do* have enough time. Now I "live out of" the affirmation. That is, I actually *feel* that I have all the time in the world, and my actions naturally flow out of that feeling. I am not trying to measure up to it or live into it, but I am living out of it. One interesting side point is that since it's a natural "part" of me now, I find that I don't need to use this affirmation very often any more.

Using affirmations does not mean that the nagging feelings of insecurity and scarcity will never rear their ugly heads again. However, affirmations make it easier to dispatch them when they arise. I suggest that, in addition to affirmations you create about yourself, you also create one or two affirmations that state your relationship with the universe. In the future, at those moments when you see yourself most truly and you see the universe most powerfully, write down what you see. These are the best times to create affirmations. You will gradually progress from living into them to living out of them.

One word of advice: An affirmation is a new attitude that supplants an old one. You need to uncover and admit the old attitude to yourself before you replace it with the new attitude. For example, we need to admit an attitude of scarcity before we can supplant it with an attitude of abundance. Sometimes we need the professional help of a therapist to uncover the old attitude that holds us down and to see where that attitude came from.

Although I will suggest some practical actions you can take later in this book, more importantly I will suggest affirmations, new ways of viewing reality. Even more important than the affirmations *I* give are the ones *you* invent for yourself. Recreate how you look at yourself and your world in ways that empower you, help you to move forward and enjoy the fullness of life. Mine work for me. Use them or create what works for you.

CHAPTER 21

SUMMARY: AFFIRMATIONS ON THE SEVEN SCARCITIES

Let's now complete the discussion about the Seven Scarcities, seven non-useful ways of looking at things, which cause us to overwork and to do many other unhealthy things as well. To offset them, we need to substitute positive new affirmations about the way things are. I offer the following affirmations to substitute for the Seven Scarcities, plus a bonus affirmation.

1. **TIME**
    ❖ I have all the time in the world.

    ❖ I have all the time I need for what's important to me.

    ❖ I have an abundance of desires, and I achieve them in their time.

2. **MONEY**
    ❖ I have ample money for my needs.

    ❖ My security doesn't come from money but from my own self-worth.

3. **CUSTOMERS/CLIENTS/JOBS**
   - ❖ There are always enough people to accept what I give, and more who want it.

   - ❖ There is an abundance of customers, clients, jobs, work.

   - ❖ I do what I love to do, and the money follows.

4. **TALENT**
   - ❖ My talent continues to unfold. It has brought me this far in life, and it will create new opportunities for me.

5. **QUALITY**
   - ❖ My best is always good enough.

   - ❖ Good enough is good enough.

6. **LIFE**
   - ❖ I am adequate and worthwhile because *I am.*

   - ❖ Who I am continues to unfold for me.

   - ❖ I am grateful for what I have.

7. **LOVE**
   - ❖ I am totally loved and loving.

8. **ABUNDANCE**
   - ❖ I have all the time in the world.

   - ❖ I have all the energy in the world.

   - ❖ I have all the resources in the world.

   - ❖ I have all the love in the world.

CHAPTER 22

HOW TO STOP OVERWORKING: THE COLD TURKEY METHOD

I often ask at my workshops: What would it take for someone to go home at five o'clock every day. I get many answers: control interruption, plan your day, say "no" to people, work on what counts, don't take calls, etc. All of these answers are helpful but they miss the point. What you need to do to go home at five o'clock is elementary: when the little hand is on the five and the big hand is on the twelve, get up and leave. The simplest way to stop working so many hours is to stop working so many hours. In other words, if you're working sixty hours a week, make a commitment to work fifty hours a week. Or, if you're going home at 7:00 or 8:00 each night, go home at 6:00 each night. And then, perhaps after a few months, go home at 5:00 each night.

Overworkers are a little shocked at this suggestion. "It's simplistic and unrealistic," they say. But let's take a closer look. Here's a possible scenario: You make a commitment to go home at 6:00 each night. At 5:59 you are in the middle of a big project which needs to be completed before tomorrow. What should you do? You clear your desk, go home and leave the project incomplete. What would happen if you made that choice? The next day there might be some repercussions. However, if you remade the commitment to go home at 6:00 that day, here's what would happen. You would make sure you got done what had to be done. You would work on what counts. You would control interruptions. You'd say "no" to people. You'd stop wasting time. Forcing yourself to limit the amount of time you work forces you to work smarter. You would naturally do the things you need to do in order to keep your commitment to yourself. People think backwards. They think, "Oh, if I could just control interruptions, control the phone, etc., I could go home on time." It doesn't work that way. It works just the opposite: Commit to going home on time, then you'll do the things necessary to make it happen. Working overtime is the reward you give yourself for inefficiency. We have all these bad work habits because in the back of our head we say, "Oh, I can work until 5:30 or 6:00 or 7:00." So we fail to control our time and our day.

This is why stopping is called "cold turkey." It is very simple, but it is not very easy. It will force you to wrench your other priorities into line to support your priority of going home on time. People who have tried the cold turkey method often tell me that they still get all their work done. So the bonus is that you become more efficient and more effective—you work smarter and do it in less time.

Cold turkey is the antidote to Parkinson's law which is: Work expands to fill the time allotted to it. If you have 10 tasks and 6 hours, it will take you 6 hours to do them. If you have the same 10 tasks and 8 hours, it will take you 8 hours to do them. The cold turkey principle is to make the tasks fit into the time, rather than make the time fit the tasks. If I have eight hours to work, everything that I need to do will get done in that time. If it doesn't, it doesn't. So, instead of work expanding to fill the time allotted to it, time collapses and the work gets done within those limits. Cold turkey forces you to take control of your time and your circumstances rather than be controlled by them.

Two anecdotes told by participants at my workshops illustrate the power of this idea. One person said that he used to work seventy hours a week and then he reduced it to thirty-five hours a week. He also said he was making more money than he used to make. I asked him how he accomplished this. He said he had a heart attack. He had a lot of time in the hospital to think about where his life was going, literally, and made some decisions about working on what counts, about specializing, about raising his fees.

Another participant told me that he only worked a forty hour week as a maximum. He said that several years ago his wife had cancer and he had three young children at home. He went home at 5:00 every day, no matter what, to take care of his family. His wife eventually passed away and he was happily remarried. He said: "From that experience, I learned I could do it all in forty hours, so I've just kept the habit of only working forty hours a week. If it doesn't get done today, it will get done tomorrow. If it doesn't get done tomorrow, it will get done next week."

Both of these are unfortunate incidents, yet the outcome was beneficial. External circumstances forced these people to work fewer hours and they became very successful in doing so. Another young lawyer told me that she switched jobs from a large law firm into a company. She was used to working until 7:00 every night and continued that habit in the new company. However, she eventually looked around and found that she was the only one there at 7:00 and so she started cutting her work hours back to 6:30, to 6:00 and so on. She said it was merely the force of habit and the fact that other people were doing it that kept her working until 7:00. Her new job gave her the opportunity to see the habit as a habit. Then she was able to break the habit.

However, if you try it, don't be absolute about it. For example, if you're a doctor in the middle of an operation at 5:59, I wouldn't suggest that you leave work at that point. You might say, "I will stay no later than 6:00 on the average every day." That means that on some days you might stay until 6:30, but you would compensate by going home at 5:30 on others. You might make a game out of it. Set a target number of work hours and see how much more efficient you get in that time. If you find you handle things well at that target, move down to the next lower target.

If you work for yourself you can readily go cold turkey. If you work for someone else, go to your boss and ask to reduce your work hours to a certain amount. There will be one of three answers: yes, no, or let's negotiate. The boss probably won't say, "You're fired for making that request." If the answer is "yes," you win. If the answer is "no," negotiate. If negotiations get carried to the ultimate extreme, you may have the opportunity to decide whether you want to continue to work there or not. If you choose to continue to work there, then you are making the choice to work overtime. You can create satisfaction by accepting the fact that that is the choice you are making. If you decide to go elsewhere, tell your new employer about how much overtime you are willing to work. One accountant told me that she worked ten months a year; she took July and August off. I asked her how she pulled it off. She said that those were the terms she requested and got when she hired into the new firm.

The cold turkey method for cutting down on your work hours is startling. It confronts you with the fact that you are choosing to work the amount of time you work. Nine times out of ten, no one is standing behind you saying you must work longer hours. We are the ones who impose that condition upon ourselves. In the tenth case, where your boss is saying you must work those hours, my best guess is that only one out of ten would confront their boss about it. You have the option of confronting the boss and ultimately not working for him or her. People who are over-demanding on themselves are over-demanding on others. You don't have to work for them.

The reality that cold turkey forces on us is that we are choosing right now to work exactly the number of hours we are working. When we make the choice to work less, we begin to shift how we operate so that we certainly become more efficient and probably more effective than we previously were.

CHAPTER 23

OVERWORK:
TRADING TIME FOR MONEY

In speaking about the cold turkey method to stop overworking, I said that the bottom line about people who overwork is that they choose to do so. I also spoke at length about the psychological attitude of scarcity which contributes to overwork. But, at any given point, an individual can make a choice not to give in to that attitude. You can choose to overwork or you can choose not to. Every time you make a choice you are trading off one thing for another. For overworkers who are in business for themselves or who bill out their time, there is a simple trade-off they can make to stop overworking: they can trade time for money. In other words, they can work fewer hours, make less money and have more personal time. If they trade time for money, they are making a conscious choice to perhaps limit the level or speed at which their business will grow. You don't necessarily have to make less money and limit your growth when you work less hours, but it may be that way initially. In fact, many people who stop working longer start working smarter, and they make more money and have better growth in the long run.

It doesn't occur to most people who are overworking that limiting their growth might be an option: "Instead of making $10,000 more this year, I am going to turn away clients and work five hours less each week." This also applies to people who are employees. If you went into your boss and said, "I want to limit my work hours to forty hours per week," you would probably receive one of three responses:

1) Work as long as we tell you to or find another job.

2) Fine, work forty hours per week, but don't count on a good raise or being able to grow in this organization. (It is unlikely that a boss would say this, but that is probably what he or she is thinking.)

3) Yes, great idea. We all need to work less hours. (This could happen!)

In the case of response #1, you still have the option to find another job where you *can* work for forty hours a week. But, again, you may have to trade money or growth for that choice.

In the case of #2, the hidden price you may pay is "making it to the top in this organization." The question arises: "Why do you want to make it to the top, especially in this organization?" And case #3 could happen. Maybe your boss is trapped in working an endless spiral of longer hours, and your taking a stand would help bosses to rescue themselves. Age is a factor in deciding which trade-off you choose. Young people just starting to work, or early in their careers, want to grow. They want to continue to increase their salaries or income. Young firms want to grow, to get established, to get out of the survival stage and to become healthy and prosperous. Most people are living on the edge. They live up to the maximum of the income they are already making and so they want to make more income to create a little bit of a cushion. The danger, though, is that just before they create the cushion, they just up the stakes by buying a bigger house, etc. and again live on the edge.

Perhaps my ideas might be more applicable to the middle-aged or more mature person who isn't struggling to "make it" any more. And yet for all of us the problem is that we become accustomed to continual growth, to wanting to have our business continue to grow, to wanting to make more money. It's the mode of operation that we've been used to for two or forty years, so we don't know anything else to do but to keep growing. We don't know how to pull back and say, "Wait a minute, what is my life about? Is all this growth really creating satisfaction in my life?"

Overwork: Why We Do It and How to Stop

This paragraph is especially directed to people who have "made it" financially. (Given what I said earlier about the scarcity attitude concerning money, not many people would classify themselves in this category.) Are you really living the quality of life that you want to live? What is the spiritual quality of your life? What's the intellectual quality of your life? What's the emotional quality of your life? Is there joy and excitement in your life? The present quality may have come primarily from the financial growth that you've experienced over the past years. The challenge is to take a look at that growth and ask if that's what your life is really about now. If the answer is no, the next challenge is to answer the question: What *is* my life about now?

This brings up another reason why it's hard for people to stop overworking. It almost requires outside intervention, someone to come in and shake you and say, "Look at this value, look at this one, there is more to life than work." It is hard for people to go cold turkey and say, "All right I'm going to stop all of this overwork," without having a clear sense of what they are moving toward. They know what they are giving up, but what are they giving it up *for?* Perhaps going through this evaluation is what is meant by the mid-life crisis. We realize we're not going to be here forever, and we start looking more closely at what our life is about. Many, though, are afraid of looking too closely. Their real motivation may be: I overwork so I don't have to confront my mortality and what my life is about.

Tied in with the avoidance of looking at where your life is going, another reason people may overwork is that they don't *want* to go home from work. They may not be happy in their relationship with their spouse or children. Or, they may not have a spouse or children. So overwork is a way of avoiding fear of relationships or dealing with a relationship that isn't working. The trade-off may be: I overwork so I don't have to confront my failure in relationships.

Wherever you are in life, if you're overworking, the bottom line is that you're choosing to do so. Your options are to be satisfied with the choice you're making now or to make a different choice: work less. If you work less, you may see that you begin to work more efficiently and more effectively. You may also start to confront some things which you are avoiding. In either case, working less is an opportunity for growth.

I have been saying that to work less you must trade off money and growth, but that is often not the case. It *seems* that way to one trapped in overwork. But there is another option, and that is to work smarter rather than longer. Some people, in fact, cut down on their work hours, yet they make more money and continue to grow. Why? Precisely because they work less, they make their time count more. They work on what counts. They become more attuned to their preferences and inclinations and become more successful.

In short, the cold turkey method discussed in the last chapter is the simplest way to cut down on overwork, to see if you really *want* to cut down, and to see what you have been trading off by overworking. When the options become clear, it is easier to choose.

AFFIRMATION

Overwork

❖   I work exactly the amount of time I choose to.

CHAPTER 24

THE STARTING POINT FOR EXCELLENCE IN ORGANIZATIONS

To start this section, let's look at satisfaction not on the level of the individual, but of the organization—the corporation, the shop, the church, the family. The question is how to create excellence in organizations.

If one wanted to create excellence in an organization, what is the starting point? Most people answer this question based primarily on how they evaluate their own current and past organizations. Some of the answers people come up with are: achieving goals, recognition, committed staff, trust, communication, team-work, leadership and so on. These are all part of what it takes to create excellence. However, where does one start? *Is* there a starting point? I suggest that there are several starting points, and that we can line them up in a logical progression.

The first starting point for excellence in organizations is a commitment to excellence by the leadership of the organization. It is a simple truism that unless the leadership is committed to excellence, it is very difficult for the organization to achieve excellence. But what if the leadership is not committed to excellence? Is excellence possible? What then is the starting point? It is a commitment to excellence by the individual in an organization. In other words, the person reading these words right now is the key to excellence in your organization. *You* are the key to excellence. If you are committed to excellence, you will create it in your organization. How would this work? If you are committed to excellence strongly enough, then you will begin to demand it from those below you and those above you. If you are wise, your demands will take the form of example and persuasion rather than coercion. If others respond, then commitment to excellence will gradually filter to the top levels of your organization. If that does not happen, then your commitment to excellence will take you out of that organization into another where you can pursue excellence. If all workers were committed to excellence, they would flock to organizations which stood for excellence. These would flourish. The rest of the mediocre organizations would wither because nobody would be there! So the individual—you—can serve as the leaven for excellence in an organization.

SATISFACTION VS. PRODUCTIVITY

What does commitment to excellence by an individual mean? It means that you are committed to two things: your productivity and your satisfaction. Excellence comes out of productivity, but only sustained productivity, and you can not sustain productivity unless the producers are satisfied. Let's take it a step further. Out of these two elements, productivity and satisfaction, which is most important? This is a difficult question for many people to answer. Many find them inseparable. You cannot be satisfied unless you are productive; and you cannot be productive unless you're satisfied. Often that is true. However, it is vital that we make a distinction between the two and ask which is more important.

Would you rather have your tombstone say: "He/she was extremely productive but never satisfied in life," or "He/she was very satisfied with life, but not productive"? The former is the tombstone of a workaholic, someone who's always producing but is never satisfied. The latter could be of someone who has been fooling himself all his life, or it could be of someone who actually was productive but didn't recognize it. What if, in fact, you did fool yourself all your life? You went through life very satisfied, very happy about how you were living, but you didn't produce very much at all? Then, after you died, everybody talked about how unproductive you were. What do you care? You're gone—and you were satisfied while you were here! It is highly unlikely that anyone could go through life producing nothing and still be satisfied. But the purpose of life is to create satisfaction, not to be productive. Satisfaction is the goal and productivity the means to get there, not vice-versa. If I had to pick, I'd rather be unproductive and satisfied rather than productive and dissatisfied. Ideally, I want to be productive *and* satisfied, but satisfaction is the final goal we're trying to achieve. Productivity is generally the means we take toward achieving the goal, but the goal is satisfaction.

Yet, there are many who are totally focused on productivity, and who lose sight of the goal of satisfaction. At the end of your life, who cares how much you produced? Being satisfied is the whole point of life. Both of these terms are relative anyhow. What does productive mean? I left an estate of $1,000, $100,000, $1,000,000, $1,000,000,000? I built one building, two buildings, ten buildings? I laid bricks for 100 buildings? I carried mortar for 100 brick-layers? What you produce is relative. You can always produce more. And you can always produce less. The question is, are you getting satisfaction out of your productivity? So the key question to ask yourself is not how to be more productive, but how to be more satisfied. This will create a balanced productivity and a satisfied you.

So the starting point for excellence in any organization is the commitment by each individual to his or her own satisfaction within the organization. If you have that commitment, you will become productive, although perhaps not in the way you thought you'd be. You will then be the leaven to have your organization become productive and satisfied from top management down. You will create excellence in your organization—if not in this one, then in the next one.

Now, let's explore the premise that if everyone in the organization is committed to their own satisfaction the organization will become extremely productive. This is so for two reasons. First, owners or bosses are part of any organization. Their satisfaction counts too. In fact, their satisfaction counts more than the satisfaction of employees. They are, after all, the ones who are—or should be—taking responsibility for the success of the organization. If the employee's satisfaction came first, then that would, in fact, make the employee the boss! Bosses are not satisfied if the organization is not productive. In fact, we could define productivity as "organizational satisfaction." The whole organization is satisfied when it's productive. Its reason for existence is productivity. So when the employee's satisfaction conflicts with the organization's satisfaction, the needs of the organization come first.

Secondly, it's not as if everyone always has a clear, precise idea of what they need to be satisfied. What it takes to create satisfaction changes. Each individual creates his or her own satisfaction. (I will discuss this more fully in Section Five.) What I need for my satisfaction shifts. This means I am in an on-going inquiry. It also means I need to have an ongoing dialogue with my staff or with my supervisor about it. So the commitment to satisfaction implies the ongoing commitment to communication. If each person were committed to communication, neither boss nor subordinate would be satisfied with inadequate or unproductive performance. Each of us wants to be productive, but not overburdened. And all of us derive satisfaction from producing results. Communication is what helps us keep a balance.

The most important attitude a supervisor can have is that everybody—including the supervisor—should be satisfied. A good supervisor should say to each individual: "I want you satisfied or I want you out. I don't want you to pretend to be satisfied, I want you to really be satisfied. I want you to find working here a satisfying experience. If you're not satisfied I want to know about it, and I'll assist you in whatever way I can. And if it becomes clear that this is not the place for you to achieve satisfaction, then I will to help you find a job elsewhere where you will be satisfied. I am committed to your satisfaction more than I am committed to having you work here. I want for you no less than I want for myself. I am committed to my own satisfaction." Organizations with this policy are not only viable but successful, and not only successful but extremely successful.

This attitude makes good organizations prosper and bad ones die. The bottom line for any organization is that people are both productive *and* satisfied. If employees focus too much on their own satisfaction and not on their productivity, then the boss will become dissatisfied. Employees who consistently favor their own satisfaction at the expense of productivity will be fired. If they are consistently fired, they will begin to reevaluate what really satisfies them, and they will start shifting their viewpoint.

CONFRONTING B.S.

The biggest barrier to satisfaction is B.S. (I abbreviate for the sake of gentility!) on the part of both bosses and employees. People don't tell the truth. Employees B.S. themselves when they complain about being stuck in jobs or being stuck with a certain boss, and they do nothing to change it. If they clearly see they can't change the situation in a job, they need to change their job. And if they choose not to change their job, they need to choose to be satisfied and make the most of their current working situation.

On the other hand, there is the question of the boss' or owner's B.S. If bosses truly aren't concerned about the welfare or satisfaction of their employees, they use the sweatshop style of management by squeezing and manipulating employees. In the long run they lose also. They get short term productivity, but lose long term growth and development. There is dissatisfaction, and the result is high turnover, high absenteeism, lower productivity, even sabotage. Bosses B.S. themselves when they don't admit they are in a partnership with the employees and that employee satisfaction is a big component of organizational success. Where bosses are committed to the satisfaction of their employees as well as their own, people will flock to their organizations. There is a high level of employee loyalty, creativity and output in this kind of company. Good organizations, defined in this way, flourish and poor ones die.

Another way of looking at satisfaction is this: There really is no such thing as "an organization." There is no such thing as "IBM." The reality of IBM is that it is a group of individuals doing things together to produce certain products and services. IBM doesn't exist; people do, desks do, computers do, systems do. The name of your organization is just a shorthand way of saying "the people who are here, what they do, and what equipment they use to do it." IBM can't lead a satisfactory existence, since it doesn't exist. The only ones who can lead a satisfactory existence are the owners and employees of IBM. It is up to each one of them as individuals to take responsibility for their own satisfaction.

It is foolish to give up your own satisfaction for the mythical satisfaction of the company, or for the satisfaction of others. The reality is that you can't satisfy anybody else anyhow. Everybody's satisfaction depends of themselves alone. You can contribute to or aid others' satisfaction, but they ultimately create their own satisfaction. Therefore, it's ridiculous to create dissatisfaction for yourself while trying to satisfy others. We ought only to satisfy others when it is satisfying to ourselves. In fact, our first job is to speak out for and pursue what we think will create satisfaction for ourselves. So demand your own satisfaction for yourself: "I want to be satisfied here or I'm getting out." Demand it of your employees: "I want you satisfied or I want you out."

CORPORATE "SATISFACTION POLICY"

A starting point to creating greater satisfaction and greater productivity is simply to declare a "Satisfaction Policy." Such a policy might be: "We are committed to the satisfaction of every individual in this organization." Taking this policy seriously would force ongoing open communications which is the source of change. My intention is that reading the rest of this book will give you the courage to declare a satisfaction policy for yourself, for those you supervise, and then to see how far up in your organization you can have this policy adopted.

In summary, satisfaction and productivity go hand in hand, but satisfaction is the driving force and the end result.

AFFIRMATIONS

Creating Excellence in Work

❖ When I pursue what satisfies me, I am pursuing excellence.

❖ My work is a source of satisfaction for me.

❖ I am productive and satisfied in everything that I do.

CHAPTER 25

WHAT IS SATISFACTION?

For some people the word satisfaction implies complacency. It has a sense of "there's nowhere to go." That is not my meaning for the word. For me it is a totally positive word. Sometimes when I am at a plateau, or "healthy coasting" as Maslow would put it, I am satisfied. Sometimes when I'm growing or achieving I am satisfied. Satisfaction is an inner sense at any given moment that "this is good." Perhaps I could use the word "happiness," or "peacefulness," or "well-being." Maybe you can come up with a better word. But the word is not what's important. It is the experience of this state that's important. I use the word "satisfaction" to describe a totally positive state.

There are two distinctions which will help to further define "satisfaction."

1. SATISFACTION VS. NO DISSATISFACTION: HERZBERG

Frederick Herzberg found in his studies that the absence of "dissatisfiers" in work did not necessarily create satisfied or motivated people. When he asked people what *dissatisfied* them, the answers were different in nature from, not just the opposite of, the answers he received when he asked what *satisfied* them.

The dissatisfier list included such things as company policy and administration, supervision, interpersonal relations, working conditions, monetary and fringe benefits. The satisfier list, however, included achievement, recognition, interesting work, responsibility, advancement. Herzberg saw that if you eliminated the dissatisfiers you wouldn't necessarily make people satisfied. In other words, if people weren't satisfied with company policy or supervision or their salary, and you rectified the problem, they would not necessarily have satisfaction in their work. They would just be without dissatisfaction.

An analogy: If you are not sad, does that mean you're happy? No—you may be simply in a neutral state, neither happy nor sad. That's why Herzberg called his theory The Hygiene-Motivation Theory. Dental hygiene means taking care of your teeth. If you brush and floss your teeth every day, will you have better teeth? No, hygiene just prevents your teeth from getting worse. So the hygiene factors are those that can make work worse, make people dissatisfied. But when you rectify them it doesn't necessarily mean that you create satisfaction. You just eliminate dissatisfaction and bring things up to a neutral state. To motivate people positively you need to ask: What produces the satisfiers—what gives people a sense of achievement, recognition and so on?

When asking the question, "What will satisfy me?" we can thus interpret it in two ways. The first is from the viewpoint of dissatisfaction: Is there anything dissatisfying me right now? The second interpretation is from a neutral state: Nothing is dissatisfying me right now, but what will it take to satisfy me? These are two distinct questions.

If something is dissatisfying us, clearly, we need to take responsibility to handle it. For example, if you are dissatisfied with your boss or with policy or with your salary, you need to speak up about it. If you find that you can't change it, then your option is to choose it—or to change jobs. But don't fall into the fallacy of saying: If I cleared this up—or if I cleared up all of my problems—then I would be satisfied. That's not necessarily true. If we cleared up all of our problems, then we would have no problems. It doesn't necessarily mean we would be satisfied; we might just be in the neutral state of not being dissatisfied. The next and more important question is: What will it take to *satisfy* us? The last two major sections of this book will deal with these two broad questions: 1) How to get rid of dissatisfaction in work, and, 2) How to create satisfaction.

2. "SATIS": WHAT IS "ENOUGH"

If we look at the etymology of the word "satisfaction" we begin to see an underlying paradox. The word comes from the Latin word "satis," which means "enough." So when we are satisfied we have enough, we do enough, we are enough. But when do we ever have, do or be enough? As I discussed earlier, the only time we ever have, do or are enough is when we make that declaration. That is, we *say* we have enough, we do enough, we are enough.

If today we say, "This is enough," then it's enough. If tomorrow we say, "This isn't enough any more," then it won't be. That's how human beings work. Today five hundred dollars a week is enough, tomorrow it's not. Today doing this task is enough, tomorrow it's boring. So "enough" is a relative term. It changes as we change. Satisfaction is a moving target.

To illustrate, it is useful to distinguish the three levels of tasks that each of us performs in our work: the challenging, the routine, and the boring. The middle level of tasks, the routine, comprise the large bulk of what we do. These are fairly interesting and fairly rewarding. But if we do these tasks long enough, they may begin to sink to the lower level—they become boring. We have done them so often that they are no longer interesting or rewarding to us. The highest level of tasks is the challenging—things we don't know how to do, that we're unsure of, that pose a risk to us. As people grow in their work they strive for greater challenges. Once they have met the challenge for a while, it is no longer a challenge. They then become comfortable with it and it sinks to the routine level. And once it becomes too routine it sinks to the boring level. As a managerial principle, when a task becomes boring, you are in a position to let others do it, to delegate it.

So, what satisfies is ever-changing. What satisfies us today does not satisfy us tomorrow. In a sense we can say that we are never satisfied. By that very same token—and here's the paradox of satisfaction— we can just as easily say that we are *always* satisfied. Instead of saying, "I am dissatisfied, I want more," we can just as easily say, "I am satisfied now and I want more. I am satisfied that I have shoes and I want socks. I am satisfied that I have socks and I want ten pairs so that I don't have to wash them every day. I am 100% satisfied and I want more." We can also say, "I am satisfied, I want more, and my future satisfaction doesn't depend on whether I get it or not." Or, we can just as easily say: "I am satisfied and I *don't* want more." You are always the measure of your own satisfaction because you are always the creator of it. This affirmation summarizes a healthy attitude: "I have what I want and I seek what I want." Both can always be true, if we affirm it.

How does one make this shift from saying "I'm dissatisfied" to "I'm satisfied"? What if you *feel* dissatisfied? The answer is to challenge that feeling and deal with it. I will talk about how later. But briefly, if you are clear about what dissatisfies you now, remove it. If you can't remove it, change your attitude. The point I am making is that the source of satisfaction is choice, not feeling. To become satisfied, choose to by saying so. If you choose not to make that decision, then you are doomed to go through life dissatisfied. You will be a burden to your family, to your employer and worst of all to yourself. The irony of life is that you get to write your epitaph right now. Some of us choose to write: "He was dissatisfied and unproductive." The joy of life, however, is that at any moment we can rewrite what our lives are about simply because we make that choice, because we say so.

Why is it difficult for people to make this mental shift? For two reasons: First, it is because we have not taken responsibility to look at and deal with those things which we say dissatisfy us. We place ourselves at the effect of our dissatisfiers, rather than at cause. That is, we don't take control by either changing or accepting what dissatisfies us. Secondly, we haven't made a commitment to our own satisfaction. These two issues are dealt with in the last two sections of this book.

AFFIRMATIONS

Satisfaction

❖ I have what I want and I seek what I want.

❖ I accentuate the positive, eliminate the negative.

CHAPTER 26

SATISFACTION:
A WORKING DEFINITION

A working definition of satisfaction is: being or moving forward with pleasure and vitality. So, satisfaction may come from just being, or it may come from doing— moving forward. Vitality and pleasure accompany either state. I mentioned the word "complacency" in the last chapter. Complacency can be satisfying or dissatisfying. When it is accompanied by peace of mind and contentment, it is satisfying. When it is accompanied by boredom, anxiety, apathy or avoidance, it is not satisfying.

Let's look at the first state mentioned in this definition, "being." When I am sitting quietly and doing nothing, is that "being"? There are different states of "doing nothing" which we need to look at. Sometimes, when I'm doing nothing, I am just watching what's going on and enjoying it. I'm either watching what's going on externally or I'm watching the thoughts that go through my mind. Sometimes when I'm doing nothing I am in an exhilarated state because of the great ideas that are going through my mind. Once in a great while I have been in a state where I am just blissful, not necessarily thinking of anything in particular but simply, being. Any of these three states provide satisfaction.

On the other hand, there are times when I am doing nothing and in an anxious state. I'm thinking of all the things I have to do, or things I should have handled differently, or things that need handling which I'm not dealing with. Those times certainly do not bring satisfaction. What seems to bring satisfaction in those situations is to move forward, to act. And yet, there are times when I am in an anxious state and yet do not get satisfaction from moving forward either. To create satisfaction at those times requires handling the underlying source of anxiety. I discuss how to do this in the chapter, "How to Handle Anxiety." So, to evaluate "doing nothing" in any particular instance, the bottom line is: Is it satisfying or not? Are we "being" with aliveness, energy, pleasure?

Now, let's consider the second state mentioned in this definition, "moving forward." When we are moving forward, doing something, satisfaction is present when we do it with vitality or energy and pleasure. The first of these two aspects is energy. I sometimes find myself moving forward with little energy, just plodding, pushing through things. This often does not bring satisfaction. At the end of accomplishing something I might say, "Well, I got it finished, but while doing it I wasn't satisfied. I don't know if the completion was worth the cost." Usually during these times I am doing it as a "have to" rather than a "want to." What's needed to bring energy and pleasure back into the picture is to create it back into a "want to" by linking the activity to a bigger goal or the ultimate reason that I am doing it. Even if doing it is still undesirable, at that point at least I can say: "This is the goal I am trying to achieve, and I'm going to get through these necessary actions as quickly as possible in order to reach that goal." So that gives me greater energy for the task and a greater degree of pleasure.

In these "energy-less" situations, it is also useful to take a physical inventory: "Am I sleepy? Am I hungry? Am I slouching and not breathing fully? Do I need simply to get up and take a head-clearing, oxygenating walk? Perhaps I even need to take a nap." I find that, most of the time, when I am not moving forward with energy, it is because of a physical rather than a psychological reason.

In summary, satisfaction requires me to look at my being or what I'm doing in the moment and to see if it is providing me with pleasure and vitality. I notice as I'm editing this text that I don't have a great deal of energy or pleasure in doing so. I also notice that I am still recovering from the flu. My body is not quite ready to run with my mind. So how am I creating satisfaction in this instance? By bringing my body along for the trip, even though it's a somewhat unwilling companion. I am moving forward with as much energy and pleasure as I find available right now. This is more satisfying than doing nothing.

AFFIRMATIONS

Satisfaction

❖ I enjoy the state of being or the state of action with equal pleasure.

❖ I do whatever I do with vitality and pleasure.

SOURCES OF DISSATISFACTION AND HOW TO GET RID OF THEM

INTRODUCTION

Before we look at the concept of satisfaction and what creates it, let us take a look at nine sources of dissatisfaction in work and how to handle them. Each of the chapters in this section deals with a major source of dissatisfaction and what we can do to eliminate it. They are:

1. Conflicts with the boss or others

2. Guilt

3. Incompletion

4. Overwhelm 1: Disorder and piles

5. Overwhelm 2: Anxiety

6. Indecision 1: Lack of priorities

7. Indecision 2: Fear of deciding

8. Lack of time control

9. Procrastination

Don't Go to Work Unless It's Fun!

As you can see, only one of these sources of dissatisfaction comes from external causes—conflict with others. It incorporates all of the other external complaints people may have about work—bad working conditions, bad pay, bad policy, etc. The resolution of all these issues lies in communicating. When we don't communicate it's because some conflict is present. Handling conflicts will take care of all external sources of dissatisfaction.

The other sources are internal—things we do to ourselves. The ideas on how to handle all of these dissatifiers, both external and internal, are a summary of many of the ideas in my Time Management Workshop.

CHAPTER 27

CONFLICTS WITH THE BOSS OR OTHERS: SPEAK UP

Often the source of dissatisfaction at work is conflict with the boss or others. People are dissatisfied when their expectations or desires conflict with those of others, primarily their boss. Unfortunately, often what they want doesn't really conflict with what the boss wants; it just conflicts with what they *think* the boss wants. In other words, they have never gotten clarity from the boss as to exactly what the boss wants in a given situation. Or, what's more to the point, they have never actually told the boss what *they* want in the situation and then gotten a response. So the problem is more often not really a conflict with the boss, but a lack of communication with him or her. Communication will establish whether there is in fact a conflict. If there is, it will make clear what the next step needs to be to resolve it.

The way to resolve conflicts is to let the other person know exactly what you think, feel and want and to find out exactly what the other person thinks, feels and wants. Let's use overwork for example—someone who is working till 7:00 p.m. every night who really wants to go home at 5:00. The majority of people never let the boss know what they want. They complain or grumble to others. They hint, or whine or express it as a wish to the boss. What they don't do is make a clear, specific request. They think that if they say to the boss: "May I go home at 5:00 every night?" the boss will automatically say, "You're fired!" Fear often leads us to irrational, unspoken conclusions. These conclusions prevent us from simply saying what we think, feel and want.

HOW TO GET WHAT YOU WANT FROM OTHERS

To deal with this fear and to deal with conflict we need to look at the "continuum" of getting what you want from others. Below, there is a line that represents the major ways of getting what you want from someone else, going from the weakest way on the left to the strongest on the right. The "risk continuum" is shown as well.

Silent Hope   Hint   Suggestion   Request   Demand   Ultimatum
Weaker ⟵———————————————————⟶ Stronger
Low Risk   High Risk

I have placed request in the middle of the line. A demand is stronger than a request. An ultimatum is the strongest demand. On the other hand, a suggestion is weaker than a request. A request requires a response; a suggestion doesn't. Weaker yet is hinting. We might place whine, complain, grumble in this vicinity. The weakest is silent hope, to merely wish for something.

Given this variety of options in getting what you want from others, where do you start? Peter Drucker says: Never take no for an answer until you've asked the question, made the request. The simplest starting place is: Ask for it—make a request. Give up hinting, whining, complaining. Abandon all hope. Either request it, go for it, or forget about it. A suggestion may sometimes be appropriate. But in the vast majority of cases, if you want to get something, ask for it. Start with a request.

However, you will notice that this is also a continuum of risk. The risk increases as you go from left to right. The least risky thing is to silently hope. You can't get into trouble that way. The riskiest is giving an ultimatum. That's not where you want to start a negotiation, but a few serious negotiations may end there. However, many people act as if making a request is the same as giving an ultimatum. But a request is a request. In other words, if you want to go home at 5:00, you go into your boss, tell him/her how you feel about the situation, why you want to go home at 5:00, and then you ask the boss if it's okay for you to go home at 5:00. You don't say, "I'd like to go home at 5:00." That is a statement not a request. Instead, make a specific request: "May I go home at 5:00 every day?" A request forces an answer. There are only three possible answers—yes, no or maybe. If the boss says yes, the request has been successful.

If the boss says no or maybe, that brings you to the next stage of the communication, which is negotiation. Negotiation takes place anywhere after request and before ultimatum. The boss may say, "You can't go home at 5:00 because we can't be absolute about it. There are some emergencies that need to be handled after 5:00." So you might say, "May I go home every night at 5:00 unless there is an emergency?" If the boss agrees, the negotiation was success-ful. However, if you work in a crisis management atmosphere, you may want to be shrewd and follow up with something like: "If we find that there are more than two emergencies per week can we re-evaluate this?" The end result of a negotiation is that both parties are satisfied.

But what if you're not satisfied? For instance, let's say, using this example, you end up working overtime three or four days a week because of emergencies. This may bring you to the demand stage. The demand might sound something like telling your boss: "I'm still working three and four nights a week overtime and that's not okay with me. We have to find a way to prevent this. We always seem to be in a state of emergency." The boss says, "You will just have to work on emergencies. That's just the way it is." Then you make the demand: "I am not willing to work overtime more than two days a week." If the boss does not agree to this, then you have two options: Accept the situation and say, "Okay, I will do as you say." Or you may quickly move into the last phase, the ultimatum.

The ultimatum is: "If I have to work late more than two nights a week, I will look for a new job." The boss will then either say, "Fine, look for a new job starting today!" or, "Okay, no more than two nights overtime each week." Before you speak on the ultima-tum level, you need to be clear as to exactly what you want, what you're willing to do or not do. The result of the communication will be clarity. You are clear that you are either going to get what you want in this job or you're going to move on to another job.

The question occurs: "Why would you want to stay in this job if you can't get what you want?" Why not move to another job? If the answer is that there are too many other good things going for you in this job, then don't give the ultimatum. Finish the discussion by telling yourself, "Although there are some things I don't like, I do like most things about this job. I am willing to accept working overtime as a condition for working here." In either case you've made the effort to get what you want, and you're clear whether you will get what you want or not. You then have options. You can't have *everything* you want but you can have *anything* you want, so pick the option that suits you.

I asked participants in one of my workshops if they had ever given an ultimatum to their boss. Four of them had, and the ultimatum was either about working hours or about salary. Three of the four people got what they wanted and the fourth person quit and went to another job. Although this is not a large sample, three out of four getting what they wanted is not bad. The fourth person, by the way, was happier in the new job. So all four actually won. The three-out-of-four ratio has held up in other workshops as well, and the fourth is nearly always happier.

This brings us to another way of interpreting the "risk" line. I said earlier that as you move to the right, the risk increases. What is the risk? It is the fear of rejection. But when you look at it realistically, are people rejecting you when they say "no"? No, they are simply saying "no" to you. In a few cases they might be upset with you, and in an extreme few it could mean the loss of a job. What are the odds of these last two happening? Not very great. Consider every "no" you get as a success. You asked for what you want, and you got an answer.

Now, let's turn it around. In what way is the highest risk at the *left* end of the continuum? It's the risk of *not getting what you want*. Silent hope is what really puts you at risk. So in any conflict situation you need to ask yourself: Am I willing to overcome my fear of "rejection" in order to get what I want? And to what extent am I willing to up the stakes in my negotiations? By the way, there is no risk level which you "should" achieve. You may have such a high fear of "rejection" that you live your life at the "hint" level on this continuum. That is fine as long as you are willing to live with a high degree of unlikeliness of getting what you want.

The point that I'm making is that many people treat conflicts with others, especially with their boss, in one of two extremes: silence or ultimatum. Often they deliver the ultimatum by simply quitting, without ever having said *anything*. Why are people afraid to make requests of their boss? One thing is their feeling of lack of self-worth. In other words, the reason three out of four people I mentioned in the last paragraph got what they wanted is because their bosses realized they made a valuable contribution to the organization. Rather than lose them, the bosses gave them what they wanted. Most of us do excellent jobs and yet we don't look objectively at our value to the organization. We look subjectively at our feelings of insecurity or scarcity, and that's what guides our actions rather than the reality of what we contribute.

Asking for what you want in an organization is the best way of objectifying your worth to the organization. Most times you will find that you are worth more to the organization than your feelings of insecurity led you to believe. If, on the other hand, you find that you're not worth as much to the organization as you thought, then you have learned something about yourself or something about your relationship to the organization. It is time to either shape up in this organization or move on to an organization that will appreciate your talents. If you go to a succession of organizations that don't appreciate your talents, then it should become apparent to you that your expectations are not in line with reality—you're not as great as you thought you were. Whatever happens ultimately, you can only win by having open communication with your boss or with anyone else with whom you experience a conflict.

In summary, handling conflicts with others, especially with the boss, comes down to being willing to communicate what you feel, think and want. Peter Drucker's dictum is worth repeating here: "Never take no for an answer until you've made the request." The second part of handling conflict is to hear what the other feels, thinks and wants. If you don't walk away with agreement, at least you walk away with clarity. Then you move to your next step.

We are upset when past or present expectations are not fulfilled. In fact, that is the definition of being upset: unfulfilled expectation. If you had no expectations, you would never be upset. When a past expectation is not met, the only thing to do is to acknowledge it—to others and/or to ourselves—and then move on. But when a current expectation is not being met, when you are experiencing a conflict in not getting what you want, the thing to do is resolve it: ask for what you want.

AFFIRMATIONS

Handling Conflict with Others

❖ I always say what I feel, think and want.

❖ Whenever I tell the truth, I win.

❖ I always resolve conflicts successfully.

❖ I ask for what I want.

CHAPTER 28

GUILT:
LIGHTEN UP

More often than not, people are dissatisfied in work not because of external things but because of internal things, things going
on within themselves. The next eight chapters are about internal
dissatisfiers. Earlier I spoke about the feeling of scarcity and
inadequacy. Now I am going to speak about the feeling that often
goes with it, one which deprives us of creating satisfaction not only
in our work but also in our lives— guilt.

Where does guilt come from? One source is the thought: I
could have done this better; I could have done this differently. I was
inadequate. Guilt never comes from saying: It's clear to me that I
did the best I could do under the circumstances. Guilt always
comes from the feeling of inadequacy. It is helpful to distinguish
guilt from responsibility. Responsibility doesn't bring self-negation with it. Responsibility says: "It's clear to me that I did an
inadequate job; I could have done it in this way had I chosen to."
But it doesn't add: "Therefore, I am a bad person for this. I am
inadequate as a person; something is wrong with me." Guilt
means, not only was the *job* inadequate, but *I* am inadequate. It is self-
negation. Something is bad or wrong about *me*. So, we need to
substitute responsibility in place of guilt, to acknowledge that I could
have done something better or differently, but that fact in no way

diminishes my self-worth.

We can make a further distinction about doing an inadequate job. Did we do it consciously or unconsciously?

1. Conscious inadequacy, for example, might be: "I chose to complete this report in half an hour because I have to leave for a meeting. So, it will not be as good as it could be." A variation of this choice might be: "I consciously choose to work on client A rather than client B because client B will give me a harder time than client A; so my work for client B will wait." It is a conscious and responsible choice between two conflicting options.

2. Unconscious inadequacy is: "I could have done this better or differently, but I'm not sure how." Unconscious inadequacy is the real culprit. It comes from an underlying sense of inadequacy: "I know I could have done this better." But when faced with the question, "How?" we answer, "I'm not sure; I just know I could have done it better." The message behind this is, "I always do things wrong. I always do things inadequately. I am an inadequate person." This guilt is totally useless and debilitating.

In the first case, I am conscious of my choice and simply need to acknowledge it. There is no diminishing of myself for having made that choice. In the second case, what's called for is to get clear about the choice we actually made. For example, let's say we wanted to organize our work but didn't. We need to ask what happened that prevented us from doing it. Perhaps some phone calls came in. Then we could say, "You know, I chose to take those phone calls and I'm happy I made that choice rather than to get organized." Or, "I am unhappy I made that choice; it would have been better to put off the phone calls until I finished organizing." Each of those choices demonstrates responsibility, but not guilt.

So, what's necessary is to get clear about our choices, acknowledge that we made them and acknowledge that we would or would not make exactly the same choices again. We need to say, "I chose to complete the report in the half hour, and I would make the same choice again given the same circumstances." Or, "I chose not to get organized but to take phone calls, but I would *not* make the same choice again."

In all cases it is vital to tell ourselves: "I did the best I could." But what if you say: "If I had been thinking clearly, I would have chosen differently"? The reality is that you weren't thinking clearly. So, given the circumstances, given the mental state you were in, you did the best you could do in that situation. It is the quality of self-forgiveness that comes from reflecting clearly on our experience and never negating ourselves. We sometimes make choices we would change, but in all cases we give ourselves credit for doing the best we could in the situation. This is really a fundamental decision for everything you have done in the past: I did the best I could do. It is eliminating the judgment, "I am a bad person, an inadequate person." The reality is that I am worthwhile no matter what choices I made. So, if we remove the self-negation from the statement, "I could have done better," what does that leave us with? Simply, "I made this choice and I would do it again," or, "I made this choice and I would not do it again."

This discussion has to do with guilt about things from the past. The other type of guilt is guilt about the present. That is, instead of "I should have," we say, "I should" or, "I shouldn't." This kind of guilt is discussed in the chapter on procrastination. In both cases, the thing to do is lighten up. You don't have to get it right all the time. Or a better way of saying it: You *do* get it right all the time. You are just an atom in the universe doing the best you can. You're all right!

AFFIRMATIONS

Handling Guilt

❖ I did the best I could.

❖ I always do my best.

❖ My best is good enough.

❖ So, I made a mistake.

CHAPTER 29

INCOMPLETION: GET IT DONE

One of the major reasons people are both unproductive and dissatisfied is because of the "incompletions" in their work and in their life. We are left with so many things incomplete at the end of the day, or the week, or the month, or the year, or our life. There's always something left hanging. For example, there are the piles on your desk. Everything in your pile is something that is incomplete. For another example, there are the anxieties in your head. Everything that's on your mind is something that's incomplete. So we need to look at why we have so many incompletions and what we can do about them. What would it take to clear up the pile? What would it take to clear up the pile in your head?

The primary reason we have so many incompletions is that we are not decisive—we don't make decisions. Every item in your pile represents an unmade decision. Every anxiety in your head represents an unmade decision. What is it that makes us indecisive?

To turn it around, let's look at an instructive model for decisiveness—a good ticket agent at an airline ticket counter. There are ten people in line all clamoring for attention: "Can I check my bags here?" "Can I get my ticket here?" "Is this where I get my seating?" etc. What does a good agent do? For the agent, those ten people don't exist. Only one person exists—the first person in line. The agent deals with one person and completes with him. Then what does the agent do, jump to the next ten? No, the agent simply handles the next one in line and completes with him, and then on to the next one. He takes one at a time and completes it. How do we make our lives like that? Take one thing at a time, handle it, complete it.

The way to get rid of all the incompletions that are hanging around is to become decisive. But overcoming indecisiveness is a complex challenge. There are many things that come into play in indecisiveness. Overcoming them means we either need to change our way of thinking with new affirmations, or to take action with new techniques. That's what I'll share in the following chapters.

What are the areas of incompletion that need to be dealt with? They are the six remaining reasons people are dissatisfied. What they are and what to do about them are:

1. Overwhelm 1: Get rid of disorder and clear up your piles.

2. Overwhelm 2: Handle anxiety and having too much to do.

3. Indecision 1: Set priorities.

4. Indecision 2: Make decisions.

5. Lack of time control: Know where your time goes.

6. Procrastination: Clean up your language.

I will treat each of these areas as a separate chapter. The ideas come out of my Time Management Workshops. They will give you a practical as well as theoretical basis for achieving completion and satisfaction. Obviously these six areas are inter-related. If you were decisive, you would make a decision with each piece of paper and not have piles. What you procrastinate on is what you are anxious about. What you are anxious about is what you are afraid of. What you are afraid of is what you will not make a decision about, and so on.

Using the techniques I suggest and/or changing your thinking in these six areas will allow you to get rid of excess baggage and clutter in your head and in your life. You can live totally in the present, enjoy what you're doing, and do it well. You can enjoy the brick you're laying now as well as standing back to look at the whole building. So we will take each area separately, but you can move a long way forward in completing things by simply affirming that you complete things.

AFFIRMATIONS

Handling Incompletion

❖   I complete what I start.

❖   I have the habit of completion.

CHAPTER 30

OVERWHELM 1: GET RID OF DISORDER AND CLEAR UP YOUR PILES

There are two sources of "overwhelm." Both are sources of incompletion and dissatisfaction. The first is external—disorder in your environment. For many office workers it means the piles of work, papers and files that are sitting in front of you and around you. The second is internal—the overwhelm that takes place inside of your head. Generally, we can label that as anxiety.

When you are overwhelmed you are out of control. When you are out of control, your first job is always to get back into control. Otherwise you live in a constant state of being a victim. You are controlled by the unknown instead of controlling the known. Your life is not worth it if you are not running it, if you are not in charge. How does one get back in charge? First, let's look at how to clear up the external piles of work. In the next chapter, I'll talk about clearing the internal piles—the ones inside of your head.

There are many people who have piles around them but who are still effective workers. Generally, it's not because of the piles; it's in spite of them. There is an important distinction between chaotic piles and ordered piles. A chaotic pile is a mess of work to do including big and little things, high and low priorities, things you remember, things you forgot, etc. The ordered pile is your top seven projects.

Don't Go to Work Unless It's Fun!

The ordered pile comes about as a result of getting organized in the fashion I am going to described below. Ideally, those seven projects should be not sitting in a pile, but sitting vertically filed in a file drawer and out of sight.

Before talking about organizing the chaotic pile, let's ask: Why do we have piles to begin with? It's because most of us don't listen to what our mothers told us: "A place for everything and everything in its place." There are two reasons we have piles: clutter and disorganization. The first is that we don't have a place for things. This applies to the piles on your desk as well as the piles in your house, in your bedroom, your closet, your garage, etc. If things are a mess, go and pick up one thing at a time and ask yourself: Where does this go? If you don't have an answer to that question, your first job is to create a place for it or to discard it.

So, the first reason we don't put things away is that we don't have a place to put them. Applying this to piles in the office, the same is true. We need adequate topical files, a filing system and space for the files. We need "function files" for things that require action. For example, you might have a "call" file for phone slips and calls you want to make, a "to call me back" file for calls you are waiting for others to return, a "things to discuss with staff" file, etc. The idea is to have places to put things. That's what files are for. Then we need to create places to put the files.

The piles of paper on our desk are a great source of guilt. What are all those piles in front of you saying? They are saying: "Look at all this work you have to do! Look at how many of us are here! How can you handle all this? I'm hiding someplace in these piles and you don't know where I am, do you? You're supposed to finish me today and you don't even know I'm here, do you? You should be organized and you're not, and you never will be!". . . and so on. If you follow none of my suggestions concerning piles, at least do this: take all of the piles off of your desk and put them on the floor behind you or someplace else where you can't see them. This will give you a great psychological boost. It will support you in doing one thing at a time, because you will only be *looking* at one thing at a time.

The difference between being out of control or in control of the work to be done is this: When we are out of control, we have an undistinguished mass of things to handle. We don't know how many things there are or what their relative importance is. When we're in control, we are able to say: I have seven top-priority projects, five middle-priority projects and seven low-priority projects. It's as simple as that. We come from an undefined, unaccountable mass (or mess!) of work to a specific number of projects. When we know we have seven top-priority projects, then we're clear that we can do one at a time and it's easier for us to pursue them in order. That mess is not lurking in the background (or foreground).

The second and more important reason we have piles is that we don't put things in their place. Or, more accurately, we are not decisive in handling paperwork. How do we overcome this indecisiveness? Make a decision with each piece of paper you touch. Each thing on your pile right now represents an unmade decision. Check it out. Pick up each thing in the pile and ask: What decision did I fail to make with this? Sometimes the decision might have been as simple as to throw it away or to put it away.

Should you *never* have piles? Ideally, you would make a decision with each piece of paper you touched, so that no piles would ever be generated. For most people, this is unrealistic. You're away from the office, emergencies happen, you're pushing on a big project—so things pile up. The principle I work under is: If I always have piles, something's wrong; if I never have piles, something's wrong. People can go overboard on being neat and organized. If you never have piles that may mean one of the following: you're not doing enough work; you're spending too much time on B and C priorities; you're not generating enough new work or new ideas; you're not creating; you're spending too much time organizing rather than doing.

There are some dynamic, powerful, creative individuals who handle each thing as it comes up, who have total control over their work, who never have piles and yet who are creating greater and greater results. I haven't met very many of them. With most effective workers, there's a natural ebb and flow of piles—with piles being absent more often than not. Perhaps this corresponds to the business cycles of the year, or the cycles of the month. When the "busy season" peaks, piles reappear. When the peak period is over we reorganize. For example, after traveling extensively giving seminars, I sometimes have one or two weeks back at the office when I don't teach. These are natural times for me to reorganize and handle what's piled up during my absence. Periodically we need to get back in control, to clear up the piles.

GOING FROM MESS TO ORDER

How to attack the pile? First, I'll give some principles and then a process to follow.

As you're going through the pile, bunch or group together related smaller tasks into one big task which you can call a "project." For example, you might put all the phone calls you need to return into one project called "Calls." You might put several long pieces for dictation into one project called "Dictation." Other projects might be called "Filing," or "Reading," etc. So when going through your piles, you don't really have 89 tasks, some of which are big and some of which are little. What you now have are 19 projects which subsume those 89 tasks. Then when you do your work, it's not a question of doing one thing after another where you have no sense of progress or control. Instead, you attack one project at a time.

For example, if you have a "Calls" project of eleven calls, when you have made the eleven calls you know you have completed one major project, "Calls." Five of those calls may be sitting in your "to call me back" file because you haven't reached them, but at least you've completed the one project called, "Calls." If you have thirty calls to return, you might make it into two projects: important calls and unimportant calls. Or you might make "separating phone calls" a first project. The important things is to make it easy on yourself to get through the pile initially. You progress from: "I have an infinite number of things to do," to "I have 89 things to do," to "I have 19 projects to do," to "I have seven high priority projects." Now there is order and you are in control—no more "overwhelm."

In addition, you will complete those projects much more quickly by organizing your piles first. Even if this weren't true, even if it took the same amount of time to do the projects one right after another instead of organizing first, it's still much better to get organized first. We get a tremendous sense of control, a sense of accomplishment, a sense of moving through priorities when we do this. Why not *feel* good about your work? When you *feel* good, you move forward with greater energy and velocity. It's never the work that stops you; it's your feeling about the work that stops you. Feel good—get organized!

With this as a background, let's move on to how to actually process the pile.

HOW TO HANDLE PAPERWORK DECISIVELY:
THE THREE-MINUTE RULE

How can we be decisive so as to both clear up our piles and prevent their generation? I have a simple method called "The Three-Minute Rule." I already gave you one suggestion for clearing up piles: group tasks into projects. The next step is, create a time to clear it up—a weekend day, a half hour every day from 4:30 to 5:00 until it's handled, etc. Finally, follow the Three-Minute Rule.

This rule is excellent not only for clearing up piles but also for handling your daily influx of mail and new paperwork. The Three Minute Rule is very simple: Take each item on your pile and ask yourself, can I handle this in three minutes or less? If the answer is "yes," do it; if the answer is "no," prioritize it. But don't sit there for five minutes trying to decide whether it can be handled in three minutes! Make a quick judgment and move on. Never presume you can make a phone call in 3 minutes. Put them all in your "Call" file.

The reason behind the Three-Minute Rule is this: Many items that we deal with are not high priority items, yet they take only a short time to complete. If that's so, we should complete them so that we don't have to see them again. That's why I suggest a three-minute time limit. If you go through a pile and take as long as it takes to handle each item, you are being inefficient. You may be spending an inordinate amount of time on lower priority items, the B's and C's. So the three-minute rule is a compromise between touching each piece of paper once and not spending too much time on low priorities.

In following the Three-Minute Rule, the first decision you make is: can I handle this in three minutes or less? If the answer is yes, you do it immediately. What can be done in three minutes or less? How much of your pile simply needs to be thrown away, and how much simply put away—filed? At least 50% of any new pile needs only to be thrown away or put away. Putting it away might involve making a tickler note to yourself to handle it later, or jotting it down on your "To Do List." Besides these first two actions, many other things can be completed in three minutes or less. We can delegate; dictate a response; dictate notes to ourselves; jot answers on an original letter and return it. We can even read a journal in three minutes or less by looking over the table of contents, selecting what we want to read and listing it on our To Do List. So, a large portion of our pile can be handled in three minutes or less.

What if we decide a task will take more than three minutes—for example, three hours or three days? The next decision is to give it a priority rating and decide on the time to handle it. The simplest way is to make an A, B, and C pile, for your top, middle and low priorities. As I suggested earlier, group together tasks into one project—for example, "Calls," "Dicatation," etc.—so that your A pile wouldn't have twenty-three items but only about seven projects. Then set a time frame for the A, B, and C piles. Ask yourself: Given the other emergencies that come up in my work, is this A pile a one-day pile or a two-day pile, or a one- week pile? Then ask: When will I look at my B pile again, and my C pile? Put them away until that time and begin on your A pile.

This whole process allows you to get rid of all the little nagging things that make the pile a mess. What you now have are three ordered piles and three time frames for doing them. You are now in control. This "Divide and Conquer" technique works for any area where you have disorder.

I have been focusing on piles of paperwork, but let's say, for example, you are overwhelmed by your house—it is in total chaos. When you are overwhelmed, your mind says "infinite." But it's not infinite, it's only eight rooms. Pick one and give it A-1 priority. All right, the kitchen—but that's a total mess. No it isn't. There are six discrete areas in the kitchen. Pick one. All right, the counter. Good, clear the counter and tell yourself: one down and five to go. When do I tackle number two? This process yields control, order, progress.

This process works even if you are over-committed. It works even if after going through it, you say to yourself: I have ten projects to be done this week and I only have time to do five of them. Whether you were organized or not, you still don't have time to do all of them. It's best to know clearly that you don't have the time. So then you can make one of three decisions:

1. Let # 6 through 10 wait until next week;
2. Get help;
3. Work late into the night, resent it, and start saying "no" to people.

Knowing clearly what you have to do will help you stop making commitments to do the impossible.

In summary, this chapter has dealt with how to handle the first source of overwhelm and incompletion: external disorder. We have focused on clearing up piles by using the Three-Minute Rule and how to get control over external disorder. The next challenge is to get control over internal disorder. That is, when we are plagued by the overwhelm of all the incomplete things which we carry inside our head—anxiety—what should we do? The next chapter deals with that.

AFFIRMATIONS

Handling Overwhelm

❖ I am in control of my work.

❖ I make a decision with every piece of paper I touch.

❖ I am orderly.

❖ Order surrounds me.

CHAPTER 31

OVERWHELM 2: HANDLE ANXIETY AND HAVING TOO MUCH TO DO

The next source of incompletion, overwhelm and dissatisfaction is anxiety. It's the inner voice in our head that says: "I've got an infinite number of things to do. I've got very difficult things to do. I've got things on my mind that I don't know how to handle." It is also the feeling in our gut that says: "I am not in control." Webster's second definition of anxiety is: "An abnormal and overwhelming sense of apprehension and fear often marked by... doubt concerning the reality and nature of the threat, and by self-doubt about one's capacity to deal with it." So it is a state of fear that comes from the unknown: *Is* there a threat? *What* is the threat? Can I deal with it? The only way to deal with anxiety is to go from the unknown to the known: to know what the perceived threat is, whether it is really a threat or not, and whether there is anything I can do about it.

The method to handle internal anxiety is basically the same as the one I just gave for handling external anxiety—piles. It is to go from being out of control to being in control. It is to go from the infinite to the finite. When you are out of control, your first job is to get back in control. That applies both to externals—piles—and internals—your psyche.

How do we control our anxiety? A simple technique is called

Sources of Dissatisfaction

"The Anxiety List." It's a procedure you can use every time you are in an anxious state, and you will get back in control. I suggest trying it right now:

1. Take out a piece of paper and pencil and make a list of everything that's on your mind right now. Make one list for work-related items and another for personal items, or simply make one big list. List all of your anxieties, worries and concerns, whether they're big or small. If you're not particularly anxious or worried about anything, you can simply make a "what's on my mind" list. Do this first, then continue reading.

2. After you have as big a list as you can make, take each item on the list and ask yourself: Am I clear about what I need to do to handle this? Simply write "yes" or "no" after each item.

3. Then look at your "no's." You may recognize that some of them are completely out of your control. That is, you see that you can't do anything about the item. If this is the case, just draw a line through that item. Cross it off your list.

4. For the other "no's," write the name or initials of the most likely person for you to talk to in order to either get clarification or to help you move forward on the item.

5. Next, prioritize your list: put the letter A next to the most important items, B to those of middle importance, and C to those of least importance.

6. Then, for your A's, identify the three most important in both the work and personal sections of your list and number them 1, 2 and 3.

After you've gone through this process, ask yourself how you feel. The possibilities are: You feel better, or worse, or the same. People generally feel better because it helps them go from the unknown and infinite to the known and finite. Even if you feel the same, you have gone from the unknown to the known. And if you feel worse, ask yourself this: If you're in trouble, is it better to know you're in trouble or not?

THE ANATOMY OF ANXIETY

To get a better insight into why making an "Anxiety List" works, especially if you make it when you're feeling anxious, let's look at where anxiety comes from. It comes from one of three sources:

1) You have too many things on your mind and you are overwhelmed.

2) You are anxious about certain items you don't know how to handle.

3) You are anxious about certain items you do know how to handle, but you are afraid to handle them.

So, anxiety comes from: "Too many," "I don't know how to handle this," or "I'm afraid." Let's look at how to deal with each of these three sources of anxiety.

1) TOO MANY

Let's first look at overwhelm from having too many things on your mind. The sorting process you go through in making your Anxiety List is the same as the process you go through in clearing up your piles. For piles you end up with A, B and C piles; for anxiety you end up with A, B and C categories on your list. You then see that you don't have an infinite number of things on your mind; you have a finite number: 8 A's, 8 B's and 7 C's. Look at your A's. You can't deal with everything at once; you can only do one thing at a time. You might as well tackle your A-1 item. Many times you get rid of your anxiety simply by seeing that you don't have as many things on your list as you thought. Our mind says, "I have an infinite number of things troubling me;" the list says, "I have 23 things on my mind and only eight of those are A's". You have gone from being overwhelmed to being in control.

Sources of Dissatisfaction

On the other hand you may have more things on your list than you thought you would have. The list may have brought out other items which you weren't thinking about. This is why you may sometimes feel worse after making an Anxiety List. But you are still ahead of the game. As I said earlier, this list could as easily be called an "Incompletion List." If you have 87 things that need completing in your life, it's better to know that than not to.

In addition, many items need to be done quickly. It's better to know you have too many things to handle beforehand than when you're in the middle of them. When during the week do you find out you have too much to do that week? Thursday? Friday? If you made your Anxiety List at the beginning of every week, you would know ahead of time how many things you had to handle. If you saw that it was impossible to do them all, you would get help. You would not waste time. You wouldn't make new commitments that you couldn't handle. You would say "no" to people. So even if you feel worse about the number of items on your list, you are still better off. Sometimes we use the ostrich method to deal with problems: We put our head in the sand and hope they go away. That's why we're anxious! Your Anxiety List pulls them right out in front of you and makes it easier to deal with them.

What's the difference between an Anxiety List and a To Do List? There are three answers:

1.   There is no difference. An anxiety list is a To Do List, to which we add anxiety. The reality is: "I have twenty-seven things on my mind and nine of them are A's. Out of my A's, I don't know how to deal with four of them, including my A-1." Your attitude about that reality may be either one of panic or one of control. The list is the same, one way or the other. You can either deal with it in an anxious way or a controlled way. You have a choice about being anxious or not. But it requires a decision. What helps us make the decision to *not* be anxious is clearly stating the reality, as shown above, and then affirming: I am in control and I can handle everything. I can handle what needs to be handled, one thing at a time. In the next chapter I will speak more about the process of setting priorities. It is the only thing to do when you have too much to do.

2. The second way of comparing an Anxiety List and a To Do List is this: An Anxiety List is the To Do List you should have made last week. When you look ahead, you have greater control over what happens to your time. Not looking ahead is what brings on anxiety. If we don't plan—make a list and prioritize—ahead of time, then new things come up and we're not sure whether we should handle them or not. The more new things that come up the more cluttered our mind becomes and the more anxious we become. When you have a list it is easier to judge the importance of new things that come up. So if you sat down and actually wrote out an Anxiety List each week, eventually it would become your weekly planning list. The anxiety would lessen since you would be in control.

3. The third difference between an Anxiety List and a To Do List is that all of your "yes's" on your Anxiety List are clearly Things To Do. But what about the "no's", those things you don't know how to handle? If you followed the instructions I gave you, the "no's" that are out of your control would be crossed off, and the others would have the name of someone next to them. So now you know what to do: talk to someone about it. When you don't know what to do, that's your first step. So now you really do have a To Do List. Do the "yes's" and talk to someone about the "no's". But let's look further at this.

2) NOT KNOWING HOW TO HANDLE SOMETHING

As I just said, there are two categories of "no's" on our anxiety list: those things over which we have no control, and those over which we do have control but aren't sure how to proceed with. With those things that are out of our control, as we saw in the Anxiety List exercise, the only thing to do is cross them off our list. What else is there to do about them? Nothing. Yet we need to make a conscious decision not to worry about them.

When people in my workshops cross "no's" off their list, there are usually two reactions. Most people actually feel relieved. Crossing it off the list is an honest statement: "This is out of my control; I'm not going to worry about it." Sometimes, though, you

Sources of Dissatisfaction

may still feel uneasy about crossing something off. If that's the case, I suggest that you communicate with someone about the item. Some of the items may have deep emotional significance—a health problem, a loved one in trouble. But we still have to ask the question: Is there anything I can do about this; is it out of my control or not? Sometimes letting go requires talking it out with someone close to you.

The second category of anxieties to which we say, "No, I am not clear about how to handle this," are those which we're not sure how to proceed with. We know we can do something about it, but we're not quite sure what. Then what? Well, what do you do when you don't know something? You ask. You talk to someone. You communicate about it. Perhaps the reason it's on the list for so long, even years, is precisely that we have kept it to ourselves. We are looking at the situation from a fixed and limited point of view which is not adequate for dealing with the issue. Another point of view is called for. So, talk to someone about it—your spouse, a close friend, a co-worker. Tell them: "I'm having a problem in this area and I'd like to talk to you about it; I'm not clear about what I should do and I'd like your feedback." They may have good advice for you. More often than not, it's not their advice that will move you forward in handling the situation, but the act of communicating itself.

Often we come to see for ourselves what action we need to take simply by talking. In fact, if you took all of the "no's" on your anxiety list and sat down with a tape recorder and talked to yourself about each item, you probably would work through most of them without having to speak to anyone else. Just take a tape recorder and ask: Why is this a problem for me? What is it that I don't know, that I don't understand? What prevents me from moving forward? What outcome would I like? Where is the stumbling block? Self-reflection through verbal communication gradually works through most problems. In reality then, your Anxiety List *is* a To Do List. For those things you know how to handle, the "yes's," you move forward. For the "no's," you move forward by communicating with someone, or with yourself. What else is there to do? Worry about it!

3) FEAR

The third and perhaps largest category of anxieties is things we're afraid of. I just spoke about not knowing how to handle a situation as a source of anxiety. Often we don't know how to handle it because we're afraid to make a decision. We're afraid that if we make a decision, it will be the wrong one, or things will turn out worse. This often comes about from anxieties which require us to confront others. Fear of making a decision and fear of conflict are just two sources of anxiety. When we are afraid of something, we tend to put it off, to procrastinate on it. So I will discuss fear of making a decision in the next chapter and other forms of fear in the section on procrastination.

In summary, just as we can handle the external overwhelm of piles or disorder, we can handle the internal overwhelm of anxiety. We can go from the "undistinguished mess" to a specific number— 17 things on my mind. And from there we can say: "I know how to handle 12, and don't know how to handle the other 5. I'll talk to someone about the ones I don't know how to handle. Four out of the 12 are priorities, and I'll handle them first, one at a time." The Anxiety List enables us to take control of our internal environment just as clearing up piles does our external environment.

AFFIRMATIONS

Handling Anxiety and Too Much to Do

❖ I have a finite number of things to handle. I handle them as well as I can, one at a time.

❖ What is out of my control, I allow to be out of my control.

❖ When I'm not sure, I communicate and get sure.

❖ I am in control. I handle what needs to be handled, one thing at a time.

CHAPTER 32

INDECISION 1:
SET PRIORITIES

One of the results of becoming anxious when we are over-whelmed with "too much to do" is that we become catatonic and indecisive: "I can't do everything; therefore, I do nothing." The way out of *that* bind is to make a decision: set priorities. The word "priority" comes from the latin word "prius," which means "first." So setting priorities simply means deciding what comes first. The point is that you can only do one thing at a time, so what's first?

The opposite, the syndrome of immobilization, feeds on itself and generates further incompletion and dissatisfaction. How do we get out of that syndrome? Let's apply the concept I discussed in the last chapter to setting priorities among your daily or weekly or monthly tasks. The basic concept is to shift into the attitude of taking charge: "I can't do everything, so I do one thing at a time. I decide what's important and do that."

What allows us to say this is disciplining ourselves to get in control. There are three prerequisites for being in control:

1) I know everything I need to do; nothing is slipping by me.

2) I have decided an order of priorities—what's more impor-tant and what's less important.

3) I am moving forward in doing things, one at a time.

Concerning #1, not letting anything slip by you, I suggest keeping three kinds of lists:

1) Your daily "To Do List" for immediate tasks. I'll speak more about this later.

2) Your "Running List" for things you want to accomplish within the next two weeks or so.

3) Your "Follow-Up List" for things you want to accomplish anytime in the future after the next two weeks. There are three places to keep this list:

    1) Your calendar—if you have relatively few things to remember in the future.

    2) A chronological file folder - in which you date and place notes or papers in chronological order.

    3) Your computer—there are many software programs to help you keep track of future activities.

These three lists actually give you a system for tracking everything you want to do now and in the future. There is no need to carry any items in your head. Each time you think of something to do, record it. And not just anywhere, but on one of your three lists. This system means that nothing slips by you. As I discussed when talking about anxiety, putting your thoughts in order allows you to work with a clear mind!

Now, let's consider the other two prerequisites for control: deciding on what's important and doing one thing at a time. How does one decide what's important? There are two ways of looking at what's important: long range and short range. When we're looking at a long range time frame—our whole life, or our career, or the what I want to achieve in the next year—it's the long range *results* that are important. The significant questions are: What are my goals? Am I achieving them? Am I getting what I want out of work and out of life? Am I creating satisfaction for myself? On the other hand, in a short-range time frame—weekly or daily action—what's important is not so much long-range results but handling urgencies, emergencies, deadlines.

Unfortunately, many of us lose sight of our long-term goals and spend all of our time working on daily urgencies. It's called "The Tyranny of the Urgent." The urgencies are generally tasks as opposed to goals. We generally label our short-range tasks as "have-to's" and our long-range goals as "want-to's." We need to set priorities in both areas.

What is the best method for setting priorities in both the want-to's and have-to's of life? First, brainstorm a list of everything you want to achieve in life, or on a given day. Don't be critical or judgmental about the items that come up; just list everything that comes to mind. It's similar to making an Anxiety List. Don't worry about what's important initially; just get everything out of your head onto paper. The question, "What's the most important thing I have to do today?" or, "What's the most important thing I have to do in life?" is a lot easier to answer if you don't try to answer it before making a list. Brainstorming means suspending judgment while making a list. The value of this is that one idea will draw out another idea, and that idea will draw out the next idea. Sometimes item number twelve is actually the most important on your list, but you might not have come to it unless you gave yourself permission to list numbers one though eleven first.

What do you do after you have a list? Prioritize. The easiest way is to label the most important items with the letter A, those of middle importance with the letter B, and the least important with the letter C. Then reprioritize your A's from most important to the 5th or 6th most important. Do your A-1 first, your A-2 second, and so on. Don't worry about the B's and the C's; just handle the A's. What happens to B's and C's in life or on your daily list? One of two things will happen: either they will go away, or they will graduate to A's. When your boss is in your office shouting, "Where's the report?" at that point you say: "It's my A-1 task; I'll do it right now." Perhaps you shouldn't have waited quite so long to give it A-1 priority! So, don't worry about B's and C's, just worry about the

A's. Don't even worry about the A's; just worry about your A-1. Don't even worry about your A-1; just do it! And that is the third prerequisite for being in control: move forward, one thing at a time.

But how do you decide what's important, if you have five things that are equally urgent? Close your eyes and pick one; simply make a decision. It doesn't matter which one you do, if they all seem equally important. Do one and move forward. If it is clear which you should do first, do that first. If it's not clear, pick something, do that and shut everything else out of your mind. Like the good ticket agent, handle one customer at a time; handle one item at a time.

How do we get into the mental attitude of being decisive and doing one thing at a time? It's by getting everything out of your head onto paper first. Let's say you listed eighteen goals or tasks that were on your mind. If I pointed to any individual item and asked, "Is this important to you?" you would say, "Of course that's important to me." Individually it's important, but when seen as one out of 18, it is only relatively important: less important than these 5, more important than these 12. If we get everything on paper first, we see that each item is only relatively important. Then we're in a position to make judgments—to pick our A's and move forward.

In addition, our list is a form of anxiety control. If you don't make the list, eighteen things that are important are all floating in your head, constantly besieging you. They keep saying, "Don't forget me! Don't forget me!" But if you've made your list, you *have* listened to those voices. If a voice pops up again and says, "Don't forget me!" you can say, "Yes, I didn't forget you, but you are only B-5 today; there are eleven others in front of you."

Let's take a look at the relativity of what we consider "important." Is getting enough sleep today important? Of course, but not as important as a meeting with a key client. Is a meeting with a key client important? Yes, but not as important as handling an emergency your *top* client may have. Is handling that emergency important? Yes, but not as important as getting to the hospital if your child was in an accident. So nothing is important in itself. Things are important only in relation or comparison to other things. There aren't any absolutes.

Sources of Dissatisfaction

You might say, my life is absolutely important. Or the sustainability of life on earth is important. But these are still only relatively important. For example, your life is only one among many billions that occur on the planet during a speck of time. Compared to the sustainability of life on the planet, your life is unimportant. Even sustaining life on the planet is only relatively important. Life has existed on the planet for a relatively short time during the ten to twenty billion years since the big bang. Possibly life exists on other planets. Even if it doesn't, life might again spring up when this current phase of expansion and contraction of the universe ends. Life will pop up again in one of the next few big bangs. Even if it doesn't, the universe will continue. Clearly, what's important is relative.

Understanding the relativity of life ought to give you some freedom in making decisions about priorities. Do you have a million things to do? Never; the reality is more like thirty-seven. Are all of those A's? The reality is more like twelve. Are they all important? No, only two or three are. Are they all most important? No, only one is at any given time. All you *ever* have to do is one thing—your A-1.

In addition to these values of list-making and prioritizing, there's a further benefit: It gives you the ability to evaluate interruptions. What if you are already working on your most important item, your A-1, and an interruption comes up? All you have to ask yourself concerning the interruption is: Is this more important than what I'm working on? If it is more important, you handle it because that's your new A-1. If it's not, you stick with what you're doing until the interrupter becomes A-1 and then you handle it. What about the phone call which is a C priority for you, but you're already on the phone and it will take only thirty seconds to handle? Should you choose to handle it or not? The answer is: Yes—choose to handle it or not. If you choose to handle it, what you're saying is, "I am going to give this A-1 priority now because I don't want to be bothered with it in the future and it can be handled quickly."

As long as you make conscious decisions, you are doing the "right thing." Ideally, the thing to choose is the one that is simultaneously best for the universe, fits into my long-range goals, fits into my short-range goals, is what I like to do, and is what others want me to do. What a burden to make all of those judgments! Lighten up! Choose and move forward!

The answer to the question, "How many things can you do at once?" is still the same: One! We are often involved in many tasks during the day and must put down one to take up another. Effectiveness comes from making conscious choices during the day. It's being able to shift with the demands of the universe. But they must be conscious shifts: "I choose to stop doing what I'm doing and to give greater importance to this new emergency." By consciously choosing, we complete what's important and we complete the greatest number of things. It's the quality of the Samurai described in *Shogun*. They compartmentalized things in their minds. When they were in one compartment, they were totally within that compartment and gave no thought or attention to anything else. When they completed what they were doing in that compartment, they moved on to the next compartment and had no thought about the former.

What about the case where you have a C-14 on your list today? It was a C-14 yesterday, C-14 last week, last month, last year. What should you do about it? You have three options:

1)   Leave it on the list as a C-14.
2)   Take it off the list and forget about it.
3)   Make it an A-1 and get rid of it.

Do you have a right to move low priorities up on your list just because you want to get rid of them? Of course. It's *your* list! God isn't up there saying, "Hold on. That's a C-14!" You're the only one who cares. So make it your A-1 and get rid of it if it will make you feel better. The point of decision-making is to move forward. The point of moving forward is to create satisfaction. Clear your head, move forward and complete your priorities.

I have spent a good deal of time talking about priority-setting. This discussion stems from two experiences. The first is seeing the value of making and prioritizing lists as a method of being decisive and completing things, especially the important things. The second comes from my being able to free myself from guilt about questions such as: How do I pick what's really a priority? Do I have to always stick to the order I initially set? Do I handle interruptions or not? The point of the discoveries which I have made and which I am sharing with you is: Free yourself up to move forward with vitality and enjoyment, as well as effectiveness and completion.

BEING SATISFIED WITH CHOOSING PRIORITIES WHEN THERE ARE NO CLEAR PRIORITIES

Let's deepen the discussion on priorities. When, for example, there is no clear priority among X, Y and Z, we often choose to do X without too much consciousness. But sometimes while we're doing X, our mind is saying, "You should be doing Y." If on the other hand we had chosen to do Y, our mind would be saying, "Do Z." And if we are doing Z, it would say to go back to X. So the syndrome is: "Whatever I am doing right now is probably wrong." One client identified his attitude as: "Whatever I'm doing, I should be doing something else." This leaves us in a constant state of guilt and dissatisfaction.

Why can't we pick something and freely do it? Perhaps, as I said above, it's because we haven't taken the trouble to say: "There are twenty things on my mind or twenty demands currently clamoring for my attention. I can't do all of them at once. Therefore I choose to do one at a time and this is the one I choose." But when we do this, we need to do it with a sense of ease and confidence in moving forward. The following example will shed light on how to do this.

I was talking to my wife and gave her this problem: "If you were in the kitchen and Jamie was asking you to come and play with his baseball cards, Ian was pulling on your leg, and you wanted to clear the dishwasher, how would you handle the situation?" She responded: "I would put Ian in for a nap, go play with Jamie for five or ten minutes and then go back to the dishwasher." I then said, "What if Ian didn't want to go for a nap or it wasn't nap-time?" She said, "I would play with Ian for a couple of minutes and see if I could get him interested in playing with cars or other toys and then go play with Jamie for five or ten minutes and then go back to the kitchen." I then asked, "Out of your three desires—1) to play with Ian, 2) to play with Jamie, and 3) to put the dishes away—which would have priority?" She answered, "Playing with Jamie." I then asked her to visualize another alternative where Jamie didn't get A-1 priority. She said she would set up a time when she would play with Jamie later, play with Ian for five or ten minutes and then finish the dishes. I then asked her to create another scenario where the dishes won out. She said she would ask Jamie to take care of Ian for a little while in the back yard and give them both ice-pops. She would then clear the dishwasher and play with the boys later. Then I asked her, "Out of the three options, which of these is the right choice?" She answered, "They're all right. There is no one 'right choice' in the situation."

This is exactly how she and I and all of us need to conduct our lives. We need to realize that we have clamoring priorities and sometimes there is no clearly identifiable "real" priority. The real priority is what we *say* is the real priority. We are free to choose, and whatever we choose is exactly the right choice. We need to replace the attitude, "Whatever I choose is wrong because I should be doing something else", with, "Whatever I am doing now is exactly the right thing to do, simply because I say so." How you get to that point is to look at what your options are in the situation, make a conscious choice and then congratulate yourself on moving forward. Get rid of guilt!

This discussion about getting rid of guilt in setting priorities is related to the earlier chapter on "Guilt" and the upcoming chapter on "Procrastination." Guilt cripples. We always need to confront it when it appears, handle it and move forward.

BEYOND THE OBVIOUS PURPOSE OF SETTING AND PRIORITIZING GOALS

This discussion of priorities so far has focused mostly on activities or tasks—things you *have* to do. It also applies to goal-setting—things you *want* to do. A goal answers the question, "Where am I going?" Tasks or activities answer the question, "How do I get there?" Writing and prioritizing lists of goals and/or activities has three values.

The first value of goal-setting is obvious: Since you can't have everything you want all at once, set priorities; choose what's most important and go for it. The longest range goal-setting is for your whole life—asking yourself what you want to get out of life. There is a quick version and a longer version of doing this. I will give you the quick version now. Take a few minutes and write out your epitaph. What would you like your tombstone to say, or what would you like to have said in a eulogy about your life? Presume that you have lived a long and fulfilling life. A few sentences will do. I recommend that you stop reading, take a few minutes and write your epitaph now.

Your goals may be quantitative or qualitative. In an epitaph, they are usually qualitative. In either case, goals give you a direction in life. When you choose what you want to *have* or *be*, you create your own life—you decide where you are going. This is what Aristotle meant when he said, "The unexamined life is not worth living." He also said something like, "You're a lot more likely to *get* where you want to go if you decide *where* you want to go." The same concept applies to very short-range planning: You're a lot more likely to achieve what's important today if you decide what's important today. So this is a clear, very potent value in determining and prioritizing your goals.

The second value of goal-setting may be even more important. Writing and prioritizing goals and activities clears the mind and calms anxiety. I mentioned this earlier and will now elaborate. One source of anxiety is that we have many things floating around in our mind. It's difficult to focus on one because all of the others are clamoring for attention.

How can we be sure that the thing we're doing right now is the most important? The way to get control over this anxiety, to have single-minded attention on what you're doing, is to make the list! This applies to long-range goals as well. We want a lot of things in life. Some may even be contradictory. Once we get them all out in front of us, then we can judge their relative importance by prioritizing. If we know we are pursuing what is most important, we don't worry about the goals that are less important. So, when a secondary goal or task jumps out at you and says, "Hey, what about me? Don't forget me!" you can say: "I didn't forget you; you're right here on my list. However, you are B-14 and you have to wait your turn."

The third value in setting and prioritizing goals is perhaps even more important than the first two. I have always been concerned about people who set goals and who move forward unerringly toward them. In one sense, this seems to be the way that things get done. In another sense, it can be a way in which people shut out reality. We are pursuing our goals in an ever-changing world. In pursuing goals, sometimes we may shut out evidence that there are more important goals for us to achieve, which would require us to alter or give up our current goals. We may be sacrificing or missing out on broader, longer-range goals, or greater opportunities simply because we are arbitrally committed to the lesser opportunities that we have chosen.

Perhaps there is one goal we can be unerringly committed to, e.g., to be one with the universe. Within this one goal, we would have varying goals which we are ready to give up as soon as we see they don't fit with this overall goal. This is a good place to stop reading and ask yourself, "What is my universal goal from which I will never err and under which all other goals will be subsumed?"

I had a conversation with a friend who left her "Samurai" group. This was a group of people who got together to support each other in moving forward in their lives. They set goals for them-selves for the week and would meet each Thursday morning and go over whether they accomplished what they had planned. For each goal that they didn't accomplish they had to pay a fine. This was a wonderful technique for getting people off the dime and moving forward. What my friend found lacking, however, was that the process didn't leave space for the contingencies that came up during the week. Pursuing these contingencies meant that she had to give up some of the goals she had originally chosen. Yet these *new* opportunities moved forward her overall goals in life, more than if she had stuck to the original plan.

Really powerful people who accomplish the most in life have specific measurable goals which they move towards. Yet they also are open to new possibilities, and they sometimes act on those possibilities and drop their original goals. In short, powerful people always have goals but are able to give them up for better goals.

In some goal-oriented organizations goals actually stifle what's best for the organization. People make goals at the beginning of the year and then are compensated the following year on the basis of having achieved those goals. Although there is merit to this idea, it encourages people to pick safe, minor goals they can easily achieve, rather than audacious goals which they have a lesser chance of achieving. What's worse, the necessity of fulfilling lesser goals closes them off to new and better opportunities that arise. The world changes, the business environment changes, the market changes, technology changes. The most effective companies are those that are attuned to these changes and are ready to adapt to them. The goals of the best buggywhip company are irrelevant today.

In a football game, if you make your plans for defending against a pass and the opposing team makes an end run, you better shift your defense quickly. The game of life is just like the game of football: it's a game. We are interrelated with the rest of the universe and the rest of the universe is constantly shifting. We have the option of continuing to play the game in our head or of playing the game out in the real world. We play the game in our head when we stick to the goals we have already set; we play the game in the real world when we shift our goals to fit new circumstances.

Goals are only a means to help us better function within the universe. They are rules that we make up for ourselves to maximize our participation. But they become detrimental when they are not in tune to the changing universe, when we try to live in what used to be the universe rather than what it is today. We reject new experiences because we are still living based on patterns that were appropriate yesterday. Yet, new experiences may give us much more valuable information for functioning in the universe than the information we were working with when we set our goals.

Then should we set goals at all? Yes! This gives us the third value in setting goals: Knowing your goals helps you to know precisely what you are departing from. In other words, goals are a statement of what we say is of value to us now, what is important to us now. When new opportunities come up which are of greater value to us, we can be clear about giving up lesser values and moving toward those greater values. In other words, we have done our homework. When new opportunities come up, we have a framework for judging their relative value. Our current goals are simply a departure point. It is valuable to have goals and some-times it is more valuable to give them up. We march to the beat of the next more compelling drummer in the universe.

HOW TO GO HOME SATISFIED EVERY DAY #1

Let's take decision-making in setting priorities down to a practical level. What will it take for you to go home from work satisfied every day? How many people can honestly say they go home from work satisfied every day? Most of us use a quantitative method for measuring completion and satisfaction—we love to cross things off of our list, to say that we completed our list today. Unfortunately, we never complete our list.

To illustrate, let's look at this question: What would you rather do— have four goals and achieve all of them or have ten goals and achieve seven? People who choose four-for-four have an Eastern mentality—the Far East I mean. The Hindus or Buddhists don't have to do a large number of things. They just do a few things, do them well and enjoy the process. It's not so much the getting *there* that counts (goal), but the *getting* there (process). I suppose it helps if you believe in reincarnation: If you don't get it done in this life, don't worry about it—you'll get another chance in your next life! The value of this attitude is that you take the time to smell the roses along the way; you enjoy the process of living. Some of us race through life pursuing one goal after the other to the grave, and then say: "I finally got here!" Did we miss something along the way? The qualitative way of approaching life is not to do so many things, but to enjoy the process of doing.

On the other hand, if you chose seven-for-ten goals, you have a Western mentality. We're more familiar with this: "Your grasp should exceed your reach." "If you have a job to do, give it to someone who is already busy." There is a value behind this attitude. Busy people have energy, they have momentum, they'll fit it in, they'll get it done. The more we strive to achieve, the more we will achieve. If we have ten goals, we'll achieve seven. If we have twenty, we'll achieve fourteen. There's always a bigger gap between what we want and what we achieve, but overall, we accomplish more. Don't ask someone who doesn't have anything to do to get a job done. There is a reason they don't have anything to do: they don't *do* anything! That's why you ask the person who's already busy. The value in the Western mentality of always having more to do than you can achieve is that you achieve more quantitatively.

Even though you may think you prefer the Eastern mentality, you probably act like a Westerner. It's easy to prove this. Let's say you make a list of ten tasks to achieve tomorrow, and a miracle happens—you achieve them all by noon. Would you take the afternoon off? Probably not. Would it be easy to think up ten more things to do? It would. Let's say you made another list of ten things to do and completed those. Would you have any trouble coming up with ten more things to do? The answer is no. We are never finished! There is always more work to do. Isn't that *wonderful?* You may have been thinking, "Isn't that depressing!" but it *is* wonderful. It's called "job security"!

Further, why do we always have more work to do? The answer is that we are the ones who create the work. It's our list—we make it up. Some may say, "I just do what my boss tells me to do." Why does your boss keep giving you work? Because you get the job done. What's your reward for doing a good job? More work, obviously. Likewise, why do clients and customers keep coming back to you? Because you get the job done. If you consistently didn't have more work to do, you would be out of a job or out of business. The fact that we always have more work to do is a tribute to our ability to get the job done. If you handle all of your current work tasks and problems, then you start doing creative, pro-active work rather than reactive work. So there is always more to do. The dynamic, however, is that we are looking at the immediate few things in front of us. We're not looking at the ten behind them. Once we clear the ten in front of us then the ten from behind come forward, and so on. It's a never-ending procession.

Given this scenario then, how does one go home satisfied every day? Get out of quantitative thinking into qualitative thinking. Quantitative thinking is: "I did everything today." Forget about that, because you will never finish everything. You can always add to your list. The qualitative way is: "I don't do everything; I do what's important."

You can finish every work day satisfied if you have this attitude: I started my day by making a list of everything I had to do. I decided which were my A items, my most important items, and

I spent all day working on what was most important. When an emergency or a phone call came up, I decided whether it was more important to handle it or to continue to do what I was doing. If it was more important, I handled it. If not, I put it off until it became the most important. So I spent the whole day working on what was important. I completed only eight items on my list, but they are the eight most important things I could have done. And I am delighted that I handled those."

Some days you might finish only three items, but as long as you move forward in handling what is important, that's all you can do. Better yet, it's the best you can do. In fact, it's the *only* thing that makes sense. The alternative is *not* knowing what was on your agenda today, *not* deciding what was important, and running around handling one thing after the other without any sense of order or control or accomplishment or satisfaction. Instead, go home satisfied every day with the attitude: I spent the whole day working on what is important, regardless of whether I've accomplished two or twenty of the tasks I set out to do. This will give you a sense of completion every day.

To summarize: In a simple and at the same time profound sense, setting priorities answers the question, "What's first?" It is the starting point from which we get control of our lives and which enables us to achieve completion. Setting priorities without being a slave to our list is what creates satisfaction. It is key to overcoming indecision.

Sources of Dissatisfaction

AFFIRMATIONS

> ## Handling Indecision in Setting Priorities
>
> ❖ Whatever I choose to do is the right thing to do.
>
> ❖ I do one thing at a time; I choose what's important; I complete it.
>
> ❖ What I *say* is important is what's important.
>
> ❖ I do what I am doing.
>
> ❖ It's not the getting *there* that counts; it's the *getting* there.
>
> ❖ I am doing what is best when I am doing my best at what I'm doing.

CHAPTER 33

INDECISION 2:
MAKE DECISIONS

In past chapters we saw that disorder and anxiety are both the cause and result of not completing things. In the last chapter we looked at setting priorities as a way of overcoming one kind of indecisiveness—where to start. Now, let's explore another source of indecisiveness: failure to choose.

What is a "decision"? A decision is choosing among options, saying yes or no, finally choosing to take action or not. Webster says it is "to arrive at a solution that ends uncertainty or dispute about." What often prevents people from making a decision is that they want to be clear about which is the best choice. They resist making a decision because they're waiting for certainty. However, they don't realize that things happen in just the opposite fashion. The decision comes first and then comes the certainty.

A better way of defining "decision" might be this: "Moving forward in the face of uncertainty." In other words, uncertainty has to be present for a decision to be called for. Otherwise we wouldn't call it a "decision." Decisions *don't* work like this: "There are ten reasons for choosing option A, no reasons for choosing option B. I think I'll choose option B." Or, "This is due today and this is due next year. I think I'll do the one for next year." Or, "Would you like a punch in the nose or $1,000?" There is no decision involved with these options because the best choice is clear. A decision, on the other hand, is required precisely because the course of action is unclear, precisely because you don't know which way to go, precisely because you're stuck in the middle. It's the uncertainty that calls for the decision. This is good news. It means that we don't have to know "the right thing to do" first, and then decide. On the contrary, we decide first and then we discover if it was the right choice. The "end of uncertainty or dispute" does not precede the decision; it follows it. The way to end uncertainty is to make the decision.

So, if a decision is moving forward in the face of uncertainty, what's the best way to move forward when you're uncertain? The answer: flip a coin. Or, if you have several options, write them down, close your eyes, put your finger on the list and choose whichever option it falls on. This is the only rational way to make decisions. I am, of course, presuming that you have looked at the pros and cons of your options. You have gathered data, received input from others. Now you need to move forward. So, you choose and see what happens.

It doesn't matter which option you pick, which choice you make. You can never make a wrong decision. How does this work? Let's say you choose option A and later on you wish you had chosen option B. Does that mean you made the wrong decision? The answer is no—you made the right decision. You made the best decision you could in the face of uncertainty. You weren't clear on which path to follow, so you chose one and hoped for the best. That was the right thing to do. You moved forward and here's how things turned out.

Then again you may say, "But I wasn't thinking clearly that day. If I were, I would have chosen B." But the reality is that you *weren't* thinking clearly. So, given the fact that you weren't thinking clearly, did you move forward in the face of uncertainty? Yes; so you made the right decision. The act of deciding was right. It is always right. The results may turn out wrong, but that doesn't negate the rightness of making the decision. You moved forward in the face of uncertainty. Of course, not to decide is also a decision; and it's the right one if you do it consciously.

People who constantly make decisions constantly make mistakes. They are to be congratulated. Peter Drucker says, "Never promote a manager who doesn't make mistakes." Why? Because if they're making mistakes, that means they're making decisions and taking risks. They are not retreating to the security of the familiar, the easy, the least possible. They are moving forward in the face of uncertainty, doing more than the minimum. When we move forward, we make mistakes. However, the majority of our decisions turn out well. If you make ten decisions and three turn out badly, you still have seven that turned out well. So you're much farther ahead than having made no decisions at all.

A healthy attitude about decisions is: Don't take them so seriously. "Should I marry this person or not?" Just flip a coin and get on with it! Sometimes this works in a perverse way. You flip, the coin comes up heads, and you say: "Oh, no!" All of a sudden it becomes clear that you want the opposite. So just turn the coin over and make that your decision, since you now have clarity!

No decision is irreparable (except one). Every decision is a fork in the road. Once you pick your path and move forward, you can't go back to that fork. But, at each instant of life, you are at a *new* fork. You have new options to move forward. You will always have new options until death. Who knows? Perhaps after death we'll have a whole new world of options! And yet we make life-and-death decisions out of: Should I go to the bank or to the post office first?

The other side of decision-making is that you always give up something when you make a decision. If you choose path A, you're giving up path B. If you choose to move forward on a project where you're not certain of the outcome, you give up the security of knowing how things are going to work out. There is a risk involved in every decision. If there were no risk involved, it wouldn't be a decision. If there is certainty, there is no risk. When you hesitate to make a decision, it is because you're thinking of what you have to give up, what you might lose. We need to congratulate ourselves on our losses: "I am delighted that I lost this client." Why? "Because I gave advice that could have made him a lot of money and it just didn't work out. I am delighted that I give my clients advice to help them move forward in the face of uncertainty. Most of the time the advice turns out well. They move forward and I move forward with them. Once in a while the advice doesn't turn out well. If I were sure that my advice would always be good, that would be wonderful. But I'm *not* sure, and I'm still willing to give advice in order to move forward in the face of uncertainty. I pride myself in moving forward. That's why I congratulate myself on losing this client."

People who complete things are those who lighten up and make decisions. They take risks and move forward—and live with the consequences. They then look at their next options. They can't go back to the past crossroads, but they are always at a new crossroad.

So in one sense there are not right or wrong decisions; there are just decisions. But in another sense, you can look at all decisions positively: Every decision I make is the best one. Why? Because I move forward in the face of uncertainty. Yogi Berra, I am told, sums it up the best: "When you come to a fork in the road, take it!"

DECISION-MAKING: YES'S, MAYBE'S AND NO'S

Does every decision have to be a "yes" or a "no"? Isn't there a legitimate place for "maybe's" sometimes? Let's take an example. When I invite people to participate in ending hunger by coming to a meeting, I ask them to make a clear decision—a clear "yes" or a clear "no." In other words, I request that they not carry a "maybe" around with them. Often, people say "maybe" when they mean "no." Why? Sometimes there is a "should" lurking behind the indecision: "I *should* say yes." But for every decision, a "no" is as good as a "yes." Either of those choices helps you to move forward with no excess baggage. If the choice is "no," you are then free to move forward with those things that are more important to you. So the idea is to clear our heads of the "maybe's," those incompletions we carry around because we lack decisiveness.

However, there are three kinds of maybe's:

1) One kind of maybe is, as I just mentioned, simply a fear of making a "no" decision: I really don't want to go to this meeting but I'm too embarrassed to say no right now, or I feel I *should* go to the meeting but don't really want to. It is putting off saying no when we really want to.

2) The second kind of maybe is a true contingency. For example, I may go to the meeting if I don't have to work that evening.

3) The third kind of maybe is holding something as a possibility but not being ready to move forward with it now. It is a "no" now, but not forever. It is still a possibility for the future. This would apply more to an overall goal rather than a specific request. For example, one might say: "I want to do something to end hunger, but I don't want to take action now. I may in the future."

In order to eliminate indecision, we need to be clear about which kind of "maybe" we're working at and to handle it appropriately. Ask yourself, "What is the source of my maybe? Why am I saying maybe?" In the example I used in the last paragraph, one needs to ask: "What is it that prevents me from saying, "Yes, I will go to this meeting"? If you come up with a specific contingency— for example, I'm not sure if I am free that night—then you can make a decision that incorporates that contingency. You can say, "Yes, I will come if I don't have anything scheduled," or "Yes, I will come if I don't have to work that night." That way it becomes a clear decision. You state the specific answer and the specific contingency, so there's clarity about the situation.

On the other hand, if you don't come up with a specific contingency and you think, "Well, I don't know if I want to do this," then what's called for is simply a decision. You get rid of indecisiveness by making a decision. You avoid carrying around an incomplete maybe in your head by simply saying yes or no now. What's behind this indecisiveness is fear of what the other person might think. You overcome fear by saying to yourself: There is no right or wrong decision, there is simply decision. In summary, the way to handle the first kind of maybe is to decide. The way to handle the second kind of maybe is to say "maybe" and state the contingency.

The third kind of maybe, holding something as a future possibility, applies to bigger decisions. For example: Do I want to change my career, do I want to get married, do I want to get divorced? These are not decisions one makes immediately when the idea first pops into your head. You want to live with them for a while to see what comes up while you hold it as a possibility. It would be nice if we could make these kinds of decisions immediately: "Maybe I should change my career. Yes, I will do it." The faster we convert possibilities into action the sooner we move ahead. Or, the faster we say no to possibilities the less clutter we have in our heads and the more open we are to new possibilities. However, some possibilities have to exist simply as possibilities for a while. They give us the opportunity to be open to new experiences and ideas which will either support one option or the other.

In summary, lighten up about decisions. God (or the universe) is running the show. Our only job is to move forward in the face of uncertainty. When you either move forward or consciously choose not to, you are doing the right thing. Get clear about what you want, and say what you mean: yes, maybe or no.

AFFIRMATIONS

Handling Indecision

❖ Every decision I make is the best one.

❖ I say "yes" when I mean yes, "maybe" when I mean maybe, and "no" when I mean no.

❖ There are no right or wrong decisions, only decisions.

CHAPTER 34

LACK OF TIME CONTROL:
KNOW WHERE YOUR TIME GOES

The next source of dissatisfaction and incompletion is not knowing where your time goes. Most people would say that it is the lack of time which causes the dissatisfaction, but it is lack of consciousness that is the real problem. As I said earlier, the lack of time really means that we want to do a lot of things, and we are not consciously saying: "Since I can't do everything at once, these are my priorities now." How many times do you say to yourself at the end of the day, "Where did my time go today?" All of those days may add up to a life where you say, "Where did my life go?" Even though you may have completed many things, you still may lack a sense of completion. A sense of completion comes from consciousness. Consciousness of what's happening leads to control over what's happening. I remember a quote from a Jesuit: "Experience without reflection is not educative; it's just one damn thing after another."

What is the best way to get conscious about time? Keep a time log. Keeping a time log really is valuable in three ways:

1) It grounds you in reality. It tells you exactly where your time is going.
2) It gives a sense of completion for each thing you do.

3) It moves you forward by forcing you to be decisive about each thing you do.

Let's look at these in detail:

1) Control in any situation begins with identifying clearly what's happening in the current situation. Scientists describe the phenomenon as it currently is. After that, they are in a position to experiment, to alter the phenomenon. So, for example, if you are not clear whether you spend an hour a day or two hours or three hours in interruptions, and if you're not clear about why those interruptions happen, you will never be in control of interruptions. The only way to get control of your time is to get clear about what's happening now. That means keep a time log for a short period of time.

2) Besides clearly showing you what happens to your time, a second and perhaps even more valuable benefit to keeping a time log is that the act of keeping it can be a tremendously satisfying tool for creating a sense of completion. When you finish a task and write down the time, you are clear that you have just completed the task. After you complete the next item and write down the time, you are clear that you completed that item. When you are interrupted and you write down the interruption and the time it took, it is clear that interruption is complete and over with. The time log is a wonderful device for acknowledging that you are doing one thing at a time and completing each.

3) The third benefit of keeping a time log is that it's also a way of shaping you up. I use one when I don't feel like working, when I'm sluggish, when I don't feel like moving ahead. It works because once I write down a time, I am trapped. I have to make a decision about what am I going to do. When I make the decision about what I'm going to do by writing it down, I'm trapped again —I have to do it. So I start doing it. If an interruption happens and I record it, then I'm clear that I was interrupted. When it's over, clearly the thing to do is to go back to the task that I was working on. If I want to take a break, then I have to write down "take a break" on my time

log. Then it's clear to me that I'm not working at that point, but taking a break. When I end the break and I write down the time, it is clear to me that the break is complete and that I must make another decision: what's next? So the time log forces you to be clear and decisive, and to move gracefully from one task to another.

An added benefit to keeping a time log for lawyers, CPAs and others who bill their time is that it will help you pick up much more billable time. One state's bar association did a study comparing lawyers who kept exact time records as things happened with lawyers who didn't. Those who keep exact records earn 17 to 43% more income. If the first three reasons for keeping a time log don't motivate you, perhaps this will!

Why might one resist keeping a time log for a week, which is what I suggest you do? One reason is simply an unawareness of the value in doing so. A second reason might be: "It will take too much time." As I mentioned before, however, when you're out of control your first job is to get back into control. Keeping a time log will help you to do that. It does take time, but the real issue is that it takes discipline. The discipline is being willing to force yourself to work on one thing at a time, to make a decision about what that one thing will be and to do it. It forces you to become conscious about and deal with interruptions. Recording the time takes only a small amount of time. The willingness to get in control is what is difficult. Probably the biggest reason people won't keep a time log is that it's hard! It seems to take a large amount of effort. But when you step back and look at it, it actually doesn't take any "effort"; it simply takes a decision to be in control.

This points to another, deeper reason why people won't keep a time log. That is, they're not willing to take control of their lives. They would rather be controlled by external circumstances and demands rather than to control them. It's the ostrich method for dealing with lack of control—just bury your head in the sand, your work, and hope that everything will get taken care of: "If I just keep busy, keep doing, nobody can fault me. I at least *look* good." When we're out of control it's frightening to look at the reality of what's happening, so we avoid it. For example, when you're out of control in spending, you don't want to look at your checkbook and cash expenditures to see exactly how much money is going out and where it's going. People who are addictive spenders simply *refuse* to keep an account of what they spend. They won't allow themselves to face reality. They just keep spending and hope for the best. Keeping a time log, along with setting priorities, is the way you get to face reality and begin to control "deficit spending" of time.

HOW TO KEEP THE TIME LOG

I have a special time log which I suggest you keep for at least a week. It is special because it records interruptions as well as planned activities. On page 135 is a form for the time log, followed by a filled-in sample log.

Keep the log for at least a week. Don't be discouraged if at the end of the first day you rediscover your log, and the last time written down was 10:21 a.m. So things got away from you today. Come back tomorrow and try again. Maybe you'll keep your log into the afternoon. By the third day you'll be conscious enough to stop, look at your watch, write down a time and task, and then handle it. By the fourth and fifth days you may be able to actually complete the log.

In keeping the log, do these things:

1. Record the actual time as events occur.
2. Record every activity.
3. Keep planned activities separate from interrupters.

On the log there is one column for planned activities and one column for interrupters. Your day is spent in doing either one or the other. There is a start and amount time for each of those.

Now, let's look at how to keep the log, using my filled in sample for illustration. In the first column, I have a start time of 8:57. If starting time is 9:00, you don't really start at 9:00. You start at 9:03 or 9:04 or 8:57. Look at your watch and put down the exact time—8:57. Then, are you the kind of person who needs warm-up time in the morning? Do you need a cup of coffee? Maybe look at the paper? Fine, that's warm-up time. If you need it, take it. Just write it down in the "Planned" column. You finish your warm up and say, "All right, I need to get down to work now." You look at your watch and you see it's 9:08. You write down 9:08, and then the amount of time you took to warm up: 11 minutes. What's the first thing you do in the morning other than warm up? I suggest: Plan your day—make a To Do List. So, jot down To Do List in the planned column, and you start making your To Do List.

What happens while you're making your list? You get an interruption. Your boss comes over and starts talking to you. In the interruption column put down "Boss." (You may want to do this discreetly.) While your boss is talking to you, you get a phone call. Put "P" for phone. Jot down who it is—"Client X." Now notice you already forgot to put a starting time for each of those interruptions. But don't worry about it. Let's say you get rid of your boss and you get rid of the phone call. Make an estimate of how long both took and write it down in the amount column: 4 minutes for the boss and 3 minutes for client X. You're ready to go back to your To Do List and the phone rings again. You say, "Ah-hah," and before picking it up you look at your watch. It says 9:20, so you write down 9:20 in the start column. Pick up the phone and handle it, noting "P" on your log and who it is. When you finish that call, you hang up and look at your watch. Your watch says 9:29. So you are clear there that it took exactly 9 minutes for that phone call. You write down 9 and go back to finish your To Do List.

You finish your To Do List and you look at your watch and it says 9:34. Jot that down and ask yourself, "How long did it take me to do my To Do List?" It took 26 minutes from 9:08 to 9:34, but some of that time was spent in interruptions—16 minutes. So it really took only ten minutes to do your To Do List. Put down 10 on your log.

You get the general idea. List each activity you perform. I have A-1, A-2 on the sample log because I presume the next thing you would do is your A-1 activity from your To Do List, and then your A-2 and so on. You capture the interruptions that happen while doing each task. Note, I'm being very precise with these numbers. It's easy to be imprecise and, as a matter of fact, you probably will be imprecise when you do this. But you need to start out with the commitment to be precise. You may need to use two or more pages to complete this exercise for one day.

I have an extra column at the end, a billing column, for those who bill out their time—lawyers, accountants, etc. You can actually use this as a billing record. At the end of the day your secretary can take the amounts from the billing column and record them in your normal time keeping system. Notice that you couldn't bill out your warm up time, nor your To Do List. If you want to impress your boss the next time he or she interrupts you, you might look up from your desk, look at your watch, write down the time and ask, "Which client shall we bill this time to?" (Then again, you might *not* want to do that!)

Lawyers, CPAs and others who sell their time ought to bill their phone time. I suggest having a minimum unit of billable time. I have heard all of the following as minimum billing units for a phone call: one tenth of an hour, two tenths, a quarter hour, three tenths. You need to tell your clients that you have a minimum unit of billable time for phone calls. Tell them why: "We bill for all phone calls, because all we have to sell is our time and expertise. That's what we're giving to you when we're on the phone. So, we charge a minimum of two tenths of an hour for calls because we find that once we answer the call, finish it, do the follow-up work that's necessary and get back to what we were doing, it generally takes a minimum of two tenths of an hour." Readers who don't bill out their time ought to value their phone time in the same way. Even though you can't bill it out, recognize that somebody is paying for that time—you!

I suggest you keep the time log for one week. Besides the control you get from keeping the log, you now have some data you can analyze. There are certain quantitative things you can look at: How many interruptions did I have and how much time did they take? How many were phone calls? How many planned activities did I complete and how much time did they take? What was the total number of items I handled during the day and the average time per item? That might be getting into too much detail for you. But it's valuable to know how many items you give your attention to each day. R. Alec McKenzie in his book *The Time Trap* says that a successful manager handles thirty to thirty-five items a day. The point is, would you be more effective in handling fewer items and spending more time per item or should you increase the number of items you handle?

After a quantitative analysis, look at the quality of what you do.

One qualitative question is: Where are the interruptions coming from and why? As you keep the log, you'll start to see. Perhaps it's the same person coming to interrupt you. Perhaps it is your boss. You then go to your boss and say: "You know, I've been keeping track of my time and it seems you interrupted me twenty-seven times last week. Is there something we can do about that?" (You may want to phrase it differently.) Secondly, analyze how much of your planned time is spent on high priority items versus low priority items. Are you putting in time on what counts? Finally, ask: Am I achieving a balance in my activities between planned work and interruptions, between doing and managing, between recurring daily activities and project work?

Sources of Dissatisfaction

THE TIME LOG

Start	Amt	Planned	Start	Amt	Interruptions	Bill

THE TIME LOG

Start	Amt	Planned	Start	Amt	Interruptions	Bill
8:57	11	Warm-Up				
9:08	10	To Do List				
				4	Boss	
				3	P - Client X	
			9:20	9	P - Client Y	
9:34		A-1				
		A-2				

HOW TO VIEW INTERRUPTIONS

What your time log reveals about interruptions may be very illuminating. Most of us play "Let's Pretend." Let's pretend I have an eight-hour day. This is not accurate. You may have only a four-hour day which you are putting into your planned work. You need to know how much of your time is interrupted, either by others or by yourself, and how much of that interruption time is really useful and necessary. We also need to get realistic about handling interruptions. If you're a mom and your baby has just messed his diaper, your A-1 task is to change the diaper. If you're a fireman and there is an alarm, you don't say, "Sorry, but we made washing our fire truck our A-1 priority today, and that's what we're doing now; we'll see you in a half-hour."

Similarly, one secretary told me she logged all the phone calls she handled, and it came to over 100 a day. She did it out of self-defense. Her boss kept asking her why she didn't get any work done. She decided to show him. In fact, she *was* getting her work done. Every time the phone rang, her A-1 priority was to answer it. So, she was working at her priorities throughout the day. If her boss expected her to get eight hours of typing done every day, he was being unrealistic.

All of us have two jobs—to get our planned work done and to be available to others. Effectiveness means having a balance between those two. Most people allow being available—interruptions—to usurp too much time from their planned work. We need to be realistic about how much time we can and should take for planned work. Don't try to cram in more than you can reasonably do in a day, given the interruptions you know will happen. The time log will help you become clear about what's reasonable.

Disappointment comes because of unfulfilled expectations. If you expect to complete twenty projects on your list and also manage interruptions, forget it; you're doomed to failure. If you expect to always be available for the phone and other interruptions, don't expect to get your planned work done. The idea is to get clear about your expectations. How much of your time needs to be set aside for planned work, and how much for being available to others—which means handling interruptions? Have the expectation to plan your day, to work on priorities, to move as efficiently as you can through your priorities and to handle interruptions with judgment. If you clearly have more work to do than you can handle, keeping your time log will be a frustrating and beneficial experience. It will make it clear in black and white that you are accepting too many commitments and that you're not saying "no" enough.

In summary, knowing where your time goes is the first step to getting control of your time. Keeping a time log is the way to do this. Not only that, but the very act of doing it will eliminate incompletion in your life. It will also help you become more realistic about balancing your time between doing planned work and being available to others.

AFFIRMATIONS

Handling Lack of Time Control

❖ I know where my time goes.

❖ I have the perfect balance between doing my planned work and being available to others.

❖ When I'm available, I'm doing my job; when I'm not available, I'm doing my job.

❖ I am in control of my time.

CHAPTER 35

PROCRASTINATION: CLEAN UP YOUR LANGUAGE

The major way we create incompletion in our lives is by procrastinating. As I discussed earlier, procrastination is closely related to anxiety—both as a result of it and as a source of it. Procrastination comes from the two latin words, "pro" and "cras"—literally, "for tomorrow." Why do we put things off until "tomorrow"? And could the solution to procrastination be simply "cleaning up your language"?

Basically, we procrastinate on things we don't want to do. What are those things that we don't want to do? There are two major sources of procrastination: The first is fear—things we're afraid to do, and the second is boredom—things that are not interesting.

If you scratch the surface of most of the things on which you procrastinate, you will find fear lurking underneath. What are we afraid of? We are afraid of new things, things that we haven't tried to do before, things with which we are unfamiliar. We are afraid to make decisions, either because we are afraid of giving up one of our options by choosing the other, or we're afraid that the choice we make may be wrong. Or, we're afraid that our choice may make things worse. We're afraid of confronting other people. We're afraid to deal with situations that are unpleasant—dealing with unpleasant people, unpleasant circumstances, or seemingly lose-lose situations. We're afraid to take risks where we might fail or lose. We're afraid of overwhelming situations, those we don't know how to begin to handle. We're afraid there won't be a reward or payoff for doing it. So, if you look behind most procrastination, it's because there's something we're afraid of. All of these situations mean facing the unknown. We're afraid to tackle the unknown, so we procrastinate.

The other category of procrastination is things that are boring. They are tedious, unchallenging and unrewarding. They take time and aren't exciting or interesting. They're just dull.

So how does one tackle procrastination? And what does that have to do with "cleaning up your language"? To answer that, we need to ask a more fundamental question: If there were no such thing as guilt, would there be any such thing as procrastination? In other words, if you eliminated the feeling of guilt—I'm doing something "wrong" or "bad"—from procrastination, would you still call it procrastination? In short, is guilt the essential element of procrastination? My answer is yes—no guilt, no procrastination. If you can imagine something on which you've been procrastinating and you didn't feel guilty about it, then what would you call the act of putting it off? You would simply be *prioritizing*. If we had no guilt, we would choose to do certain things rather than others, be satisfied with the choice and not worry about what we're choosing *not* to do. We'd simply say: "Here's something that's boring or that I'm afraid to do, and I choose *not* to do it! I don't procrastinate; I prioritize."

Let's take a closer look at guilt. What is guilt? In the chapter "Guilt: Lighten Up," I spoke about guilt as a sense of inadequacy about past actions. Now, I want to speak about it concerning future actions. In this context, guilt is a voice that says, "I *should* (or I *shouldn't*) do something." Where does that voice come from? It comes from either other people or myself. For example, "My boss told me I should do this and I haven't done it; I should do it." Or, "I have made the decision to do this and haven't done it; I should do it." But if we look more closely at the "shoulds" we carry inside of our heads, they really go back earlier in life to other people—primarily our parents—telling us what we should or shouldn't do.

Sources of Dissatisfaction

We incorporated these external "shoulds," and they become internal. We adopt them as our own way of thinking.

I never realized how many "shoulds" I grew up with. It is only recently that I came to realize that there really are no "shoulds" in life. There is nothing that I absolutely "should" do. There are simply decisions and consequences. This insight came to me very powerfully one morning. I was shaving and feeling great; five minutes later I was doing some stretching exercises and feeling terrible. I asked myself, "What happened in the last five minutes that caused me to go from feeling great to feeling terrible?" Nothing external happened, so it was something inside my head. What I discovered was that my mind got into a "should-shouldn't" conversation. That is, should I or shouldn't I enroll in a particular seminar. This may seem a trivial decision to you—and it was. But it was a big deal for me simply because of conversation going on in my head.

Once I recognized that I was having this "should-shouldn't" conversation it became very simple: There was no should or shouldn't. I was free to enroll or not to enroll. Of course, I was always free to enroll or not to enroll. But I didn't see that because I had become frozen and distressed. I didn't realize until then that this state came about simply because I was having a should-shouldn't conversation in my head. I also recognized that was a pattern for me. Immediately after that experience I caught myself several times being frozen in a should-shouldn't conversation, and by simply recognizing what was happening I was freed from it. I then saw clearly that I was free to choose one way or the other. There are no shoulds or shouldn'ts; only decisions and consequences.

Where do these "shoulds" and "shouldn'ts" come from? Ultimately they go back to how we think other people will react: They will be pleased or they will be upset with me. Clearly, the most powerful people who were or could be upset with us were our parents. But many of us pass into adult life still under the bondage of parental shoulds or shouldn'ts. The reality for most adults is that no one is going to hit you or yell at you if you do or don't do something. Maybe a few people will criticize you. So what? When others start to tell you what you should do, you can simply say:

"Don't 'should' on me!"

So I suggest that whenever you are tempted to "should" on yourself, just eliminate that word from your vocabulary. There are no "shoulds" in life. Replace it with: "I choose to do this or I choose not to." So perhaps overcoming procrastination *is* simply a matter of cleaning up your language.

This may sound unrealistic at first, but let's take a closer look. In the first place, we don't have to listen to what others say we should do. We don't have to listen to our government or our mother or society or our boss. To understand this, let's look at these shoulds as requests rather than as coercion from others. There are, of course, consequences for not accepting the requests of others. The consequences may be more or less serious. For example, there are more serious consequences in not accepting the IRS' request that you pay your taxes than in your spouse's request to take out the garbage. Yet the truth is, we are not coerced into doing anything. We simply have options and consequences. Freedom doesn't mean we can do anything we want with no consequences. What it really means is that we have options; we are free to choose one option with its consequences or the other option with its consequences.

THE KEY TO LIFE: DON'T DO ANY "HAVE TO'S"; JUST DO "WANT TO'S"

Another way to look at this concept is to compare "have to's" and "want to's." I said earlier that long range goals are usually "want to's," things we want to do; and short range goals or tasks are often "have to's." Now I want to take this a step further and give you what I call in my workshops the *key* to life. Here is the key to life, which I am going to give you as a reward for having read this far: Never do any have to's; only do want to's. That is, don't act out of shoulds, or musts, or have to's; only do what you *want* to do.

At first this seems unrealistic. However, if you look at it more closely, there is, in fact, nothing in life we *have to* do. I take that back. There is one thing which everyone has to do—die. We don't even have to live. We can end it right now! But we all have to die. Other than that, there are no have to's in life.

So, how does one do only want to's and never have to's? Here's a dialogue to shed light on the proposition:

"I don't *want* to work; I have to."
"So stop working."
"But I need to eat."
"You don't have to."
"I want to eat."
"You want to eat?"
"Yes."
"So you work in order to be able to buy food because you want to eat?"
"Yes."
"So you really want to work then."
"No, I don't want to; I *have to.*"
"So, don't do it."
"But I'll starve."
"You don't want to starve; you want to eat?"
"Yes."
"What does it take for you to eat, which you want to do?"
"Work."
"So, do what it takes to do what you want, to eat. You need to admit to yourself that working is an integral part of obtaining food so you can eat, which you want to do. If you want the goal, you want the means to achieving that goal. So you really want to work because you want what your work produces, right?"
"Yes."
"So stop complaining. You're doing what you want."

We really need to confront ourselves rigorously about what we say we have to do. One of the reasons people are dissatisfied in work or in life is that they think they are controlled by forces outside themselves. The reality is, we are doing what we do because we really want to. There is some ultimate goal or end result to what we're doing, which we want. Sometimes we're schizophrenic: I want the end result, but I don't want to do what it takes to get there. You will get more pleasure out of life by clearly confronting what you have to do and linking it back to something that you want. That is, actually change a have to back into a want to. If you are doing have to's which you can't link back to a want to, then stop doing them. When confronted with a have to, either don't do it or make it a want to.

One woman with whom I discussed this concept said that she had to work. I said, "Would you be able to survive financially if you didn't work?" She said, "Yes, my husband makes enough to support us." I said, "Well, what would you do if you didn't work?" She said, "I don't know." It was the first time, it seemed, that she had considered that she didn't really *have to* work. Perhaps in truth she really *wanted* to work and didn't do it out of necessity, but she had never thought about it. So, the key to life is to only do want to's, never have to's. As I said in talking about *should's*—a synonym for *have to's*—you are totally free to choose to do whatever you want and to accept the consequences that go with the choice.

By the way, if you're only working to *make a living*, you're missing the point of life. Later in the book I'll talk about working to make a difference, rather than just to make a living.

How does one handle guilt then, when you move out of the should's and have to's in your life and into the want to's? It's very simple: Just take responsibility for each action in your life and admit that you're doing it not because you have to or should but because you want to—you choose to. A powerful technique for handling anything that you're procrastinating on, any task that you feel guilt about, anything you're saying *I should* or *I have to* about, is this: Simply ask yourself *why* you have to or should do it. Look at the reasons, and choose to do it, or choose not to. If you choose to do it, affirm it positively: I *want* to do this! If you choose not to, don't do it.

I suspect we would have a much healthier society if people were clear that they always have freedom to choose whatever they want, and in fact are choosing to do what they want right now. Much anti-social behavior comes from people reacting to society. In other words, society or their parents tell them what they should do and should not do, and they live a life of reacting against that. They don't come to the point of freely asking themselves: What is it that *I* want to do? What is it that *I* choose to do? If they did they would then see that often they actually *want* to do what others are "forcing" them to do. That realization allows one to live life as a choice rather than a reaction.

Looking a little more closely at want to's, we see there are two kinds: short-range want to's—what I feel like doing in the moment —and long-range want to's. Children live for the immediate moment. However, as we mature in life we give up short-range want to's for the sake of long-range want to's. In other words, we see that although doing something on a whim or immediate desire or feeling might be temporarily satisfactory, it may create longer-range results that we don't want. As we see or actually experience the negative consequences, we become more self-regulating and begin to balance short-range want to's with long-range want to's. Our life becomes more integrated and we see that we actually are doing exactly what we want to do.

This discussion is not simply a discussion about procrastina-tion; it's a discussion about the essence of what it means to be human. We all come into this world as totally helpless infants, and in growing up we acquire thousands of musts and should's and have to's in our lives. In fact, we wouldn't continue to exist unless we acquired them. ("Too bad if your freedom gets impaired; you're not running out into a busy street.")

Our real maturing into humanity takes place when we reevalu-ate the have to's, the rules that we have created in life or that have been created for us, and we make a conscious decision as to whether we really want to follow them or not. It is only when we are functioning out of want to's, when we are freely choosing what we want in life, that we become fully adult, that we actually become the creators of our own lives. Saying that I must, should, or have to is an abdication of responsibility. It's placing the responsibility of our actions outside of ourselves, as if we're being coerced into doing things. Fully functioning adults take responsibility for all actions: I do this out of choice; I *want to* do it.

Applying this idea to raising children seems to mean: Give them the freedom to choose dumb want to's now, that is, to make choices you wouldn't make. My suspicion is that people who don't fit into society—law-breakers, addicts, etc.—are those who are still in rebellion. They are still fighting against what they see as externally imposed rules, and they have never had the opportunity to freely look at what it is that they themselves want. Children need to be shown consequences, then given freedom in making what-ever choices they want. The earlier they can begin making choices, the earlier they begin to make mistakes and thus to learn. They begin to choose those things that are beneficial to them in the long run. As adults, we, too, should give ourselves permission to make free choices, whether they're dumb or not, and to learn from them. Perhaps life is fundamentally the Grand Experiment.

The way to get out of procrastinating is to examine all of the have to's, the things that you say you should do, and bring them back to want to's. Give yourself absolute freedom to do or not to do whatever you want to. When you have conflicting want to's, give yourself the freedom to choose one and give up the other. When you have many want to's, you can only pick one at a time; so choose the "want to" that you want to! It is in being decisive, in choosing clearly, that we clear the debris out of our heads. We need to clear all of the shoulds and have to's out of our head so that we can live totally in the present, totally in the want to that we're doing now. In reality, what we are doing now is all that exists. The past and future don't exist. But we deprive ourselves of living in the present because of all the should have's (past) and shoulds and have to's (future) we're carrying around. The way to do *the* best is to do *your* best at whatever your doing right now.

CLEANING UP YOUR LANGUAGE

The first thing to do about procrastination, guilt and have to's is to clean up your language and become more precise in speaking about things. For example, one way that people relate to procras-tinating is what I call name-calling or beating yourself up. They say, "I procrastinate because I am lazy, unmotivated, undisciplined, lack self-control, etc." I suggest that none of these words are useful, and that they are all forms of circular reasoning.

Here's how the circular reasoning works:

> I don't do something.
> Why?
> I am lazy.
> What is the evidence that you're lazy?
> I don't do things I think I should do.

Sources of Dissatisfaction

Why don't you do those things?
Because I'm lazy.

So the word "lazy" is just another way of saying, "I don't do things I think I should do." It would be more accurate and just as meaningful to say, "I don't do certain things because I don't do certain things." The word "lazy" adds nothing new to the conversation except self-criticism. That is, it adds the idea that something is wrong with me: I "should" do it, and I'm bad for not doing it. Self-condemnation is the only thing that words such as "lazy," "unmotivated," "undisciplined," etc. add to the conversation. More accurately, they really don't add to the conversation; they detract from it. When you are tempted to use such words, just eliminate them from your vocabulary.

In addition, those "bad" words are a cop-out. We pretend there is some "thing"—laziness—inside of us that prevents us from doing something. We focus then on how to get rid of this "thing." Once the "thing" is gone, then we can move forward. But since there is no such "thing" as laziness, there is nothing to battle or get rid of. Our inventing it is a convenient way of sliding out of responsibility. We can waste time trying to solve the non-existent problem of "laziness" instead of taking responsibility for our choices. The responsible thing to say is: "I don't do this because I choose not to." To change your life, just change your vocabulary. Instead of saying: "I'm lazy, unmotivated, etc.," simply say, "I choose not to do this."

Secondly, you should get rid of the word "should" in your vocabulary. (See how hard it is to do that!) If the should is coming from outside, from someone like me, say: "I heard what you want me to do, and I choose to do it (or not do it)." If the should comes from inside your head, say: "I am free to choose. There is no *right* choice. Whatever I choose is the right choice. This is what I choose."

Now that we're getting rid of words that aren't useful, let's get rid of the word "procrastination" itself. It has the same value as words like "lazy." It adds nothing to the conversation except self-criticism. We pretend that it has reality, that it is a "thing" that prevents us from doing something. The reality, though, is this: "Here is something that is boring, and I choose not to do it now."

Don't Go to Work Unless It's Fun!

Or, "Here is something I'm afraid to do, and I choose not to do it." There isn't any right or wrong, good or bad, about it. Changing our language and getting rid of the word "procrastination" will enable us to speak more honestly and act more freely. When you are tempted to say, "I'm procrastinating," instead say: "I have not given this task priority for two weeks. I will (or will not) now give it priority and do it." Procrastinate proudly! Whoops, I mean, prioritize proudly!

Finally, let's take language clearance one step further. I now suggest that we get rid of the word "fear" as well. Just as these other words are concepts which we attach to situations, fear also is a concept which bears looking into. What does *fear* mean? Perhaps a better way to phrase the question is: What is present when we use the word fear? The answer is usually one or more of the following:

1. Bodily sensations (sweaty palms, etc.)
2. A thought that anticipates a negative outcome (I might fail, etc.)
3. A memory of a past similar situation where there was a negative outcome

So instead of saying "I am afraid," it would be more accurate to say: "I have these body sensations, I have this thought and I have this memory." For example, if you were "afraid" to bring something up with your boss, you might say, "I have a fluttering sensation in my stomach; I have the thought that, if I bring this up, it may hurt my chances for promotion or I may even lose my job; I have a memory of my father yelling at me when I suggested something like this to him." Most often, in reality, we are not aware of the third element, memory. Often, we are not aware of the first element, bodily sensations, or they may not even be present. And often we just haven't verbalized the second element, the thought that anticipates a negative outcome. It is there, but we haven't consciously verbalized it.

The trick to overcoming fear is to identify, as explicitly as possible, what is present when we are tempted to use this word. In other words, don't use the word *fear*, but identify what is present: What is the bodily sensation, the thought of negative outcome, and the memory you are having? The most important is the second element: "What is the negative thought I am having?" Once you are able to say, "My thought is that I might lose my job," then you are in a position to deal with the thought and ask, "Is the thought accurate? What are the odds of this outcome happening? What is the potential benefit of my saying what I think? Am I willing to take the risk?" It simply becomes a decision in which we are free to decide to move forward with the action or not. By the way, there are no *should's* about overcoming fear. If you are afraid, you don't *have to* move ahead in spite of it. You don't *have to* take the risk. You can say: "I'm having these thoughts and feelings about a possible negative outcome, so I choose not to take the risk." That would be the correct choice. On the other hand, if you said, "I choose to take this risk" then *that* would be the correct choice.

So when we eliminate the *shoulds* in our life, we simply live a life of decisions and consequences. We have no guilt and therefore we don't procrastinate. We are simply choosing to give higher priority to one thing over another thing. In short we say, "I don't procrastinate, I prioritize."

AFFIRMATIONS

Handling Procrastination

For Useless Words Like
Lazy, Unmotivated, Undisciplined

❖ I choose to do what I do, and I choose not to do what I don't do.

For Shoulds, Have To's, Musts

❖ I always do what I want to do.

❖ I always do what I choose to do.

❖ I never do "have to's"; I only do "want to's."

For Procrastination

❖ I don't procrastinate, I prioritize.

❖ I have chosen to do one thing before another thing.

For Fear

❖ I am having these thoughts and bodily sensations concerning this situation. I am free to choose.

For Guilt

❖ I did the best I could do.

❖ I always do the best I can.

❖ What I do is best.

SECTION FIVE
**HOW TO
CREATE
SATISFACTION**

CHAPTER 36

*SATISFACTION:
AN OVERVIEW*

Let's review what's been said about satisfaction so far in this book. In Section Two we looked at overwork and the Seven Scarcities: It is the feeling of scarcity or inadequacy that causes us to overwork and that causes dissatisfaction in general. The answer Section Two gave on how to create satisfaction is: Shift your attitude by affirming that I have enough, I do enough, I am enough right now. This is probably the simplest and most profound answer to the question of how to create satisfaction: Create satisfaction by declaring you are satisfied with what is. I will further expand this thought in upcoming Chapter 3, "Have What You Choose Or Choose What You Have."

In Section Three, I suggested that the starting place for excellence in the workplace was a commitment by each individual to his or her own satisfaction and to the satisfaction of those who work in the organization. I then created a working definition of the word satisfaction: Being or moving forward with pleasure and vitality. So the next logical question is: How does one "be" or "do" with pleasure and vitality?

That brought us to Section Four, Sources of Dissatisfaction and How to Get Rid Of Them. In Section Four we looked at the negative side of the question—the major causes of *dis*satisfaction and how to deal with them. We looked at the "doing" aspect of creating satisfaction as well as many attitude shifts which create new ways of "being" satisfied.

In this section we will explore the positive side of the question: what creates satisfaction? I will give you my seven answers which mostly involve "being," and a set of answers from others, which mostly involve "doing," These answers affirm ways of looking at life and at work which create satisfaction.

TAKING CARE OF NUMERO UNO

Before looking at the question "what creates satisfaction?" let's look at a more basic question: is it self-centered or selfish to be looking for your own satisfaction? The answer is clearly no. For example, those people who are concerned about the satisfaction of others, in truth get their own satisfaction in life from serving others. If they don't, they ought not to create dissatisfaction in their life by trying to create satisfaction in someone else's life. Everything comes around. From one point of view, God, looking down on the universe, does not want one person to be dissatisfied in order to satisfy another person. He wants all people satisfied. For example: God looks down on A and B. A helps B to be satisfied, but this creates dissatisfaction for A. God says, "Hey, wait a minute. I want both A *and* B to be satisfied. But A isn't satisfied. Something's wrong. This isn't the way I want things."

One of the faults in this scenario is the presumption that A can create satisfaction for B in the first place. As Ricky Nelson once sang, "You can't please everyone, so you've got to please yourself." The responsibility for each person's satisfaction lies with that person. This isn't a world where each person's purpose is to create satisfaction for another and not for themselves. Rather, each one of us needs to take responsibility to create our own satisfaction. If serving others creates satisfaction, then do it. Otherwise, you aren't really serving them. In fact, you are becoming a model for dissatisfaction in the world. What you are saying is, "It's okay for me to be dissatisfied to try to satisfy you." This doesn't serve anybody. It's like people who live in "bad" marriages for the sake of their children. What they become is role models for their children on how to have unsuccessful marriages. The children grow up with

How to Create Satisfaction

the concept that this is what marriage is about. It's about pretending that things are working, but there is really no joy or satisfaction in marriage. Likewise, if everyone followed the example, "It's O.K. for me to be dissatisfied," everybody would be dissatisfied!

Does this mean: Don't bother serving others? Of course not. Serving others is one of the most profound sources of satisfaction. Parenting children through all the stages from absolute dependence in infancy to independence in adulthood is one of life's most rewarding activities. On the other hand it can be the most trying. But the bottom line is that it must be satisfying. If parenting your children is not satisfying to you, let someone else who really wants children adopt them. Otherwise, the message you give is, "You are not someone who it is satisfying to live with; you are someone to be endured." Of course, if you have this attitude you might also get help from a psychotherapist or counsellor to discover what creates this attitude in you and how you can shift it. Serving others, including children, needs to be a source of satisfaction and pleasure, not a sacrifice and burden.

In summary, it is not selfish to seek your own satisfaction. The only way everyone in the world will become satisfied is through a commitment to self-sufficiency for one's self and to supporting others to create their own self-sufficiency. The first step to creating satisfaction in the world is to make a commitment to your own satisfaction.

The next question to ask is, what is the difference between being committed to your own satisfaction and being selfish? Is there any such thing as selfishness? Our first job in society is to become an adult, to grow up. What that means is to become self-reliant and independent. We don't need anyone to take care of us—we take care of ourselves. The next stage is to share what we have with others so that they too can become independent. Achieving independence and sharing are both sources of satisfaction. Selfishness comes about when we operate out of an attitude of scarcity. We really have what we need but we don't think we do, so we try to draw more and more to ourselves. I have talked about this attitude and how to overcome it in Section Two.

In summary, to pursue satisfaction is really the antithesis of selfishness. It means to honestly seek what you need. When you request what you need from others, you naturally share what you have with others.

AFFIRMATION

Satisfaction

❖ I assure satisfaction for others by creating it for myself.

CHAPTER 37

THE NATURE
OF WORK

In Section One of this book, I lamented the fact that people estimate that 66% of the American workforce are not satisfied in their work. Whether that's true or people just think it's true, the figure is shocking. It leads us to ask the question: Is work inherently dissatisfying?

To answer that, I will tell you a story: I love to plant wheat. I love to watch it grow. I love to keep the weeds out so it can grow. I love to gather it and separate the wheat from the chaff. I love to mill it into flour. I love to bake the flour into bread. I love to eat the bread and give it to my children.

What I really love is the fact that I don't have to do any of these things except the last one. I love it that somebody else does it all for me and that I can go to the store and buy the bread. I am delighted that we have stores. I am delighted that we have trucks that bring bread to the stores. I am delighted that we have companies that make the wrappers to put the bread in. I am delighted that somebody builds roads so that the trucks can bring the bread to the store and so my car can get there also. I am delighted that I have a car. I am delighted that I have fenders on my car. I am delighted that the fenders don't fall off. I am delighted that a welder welded the fenders on. (Do auto workers still weld fenders?) I am delighted that somebody made the welding gun.

I am delighted that the world is structured in this way: Each one of us can do what we are good at and enjoy doing. We get paid for it, and we can buy the fruits of the labor of others who are doing what they are good at and enjoy doing. In this way, we all enjoy the fruits of the universe in a thousand times more abundance than trying to produce it all individually. It would be impossible for me to be an expert in planting and reaping and milling and baking and transporting goods and building roads, etc. Each of us can specialize in a little piece of productivity and do an excellent job in that piece. That is one reason all work is inherently satisfying. It allows each of us to do what we're good at and enjoy doing.

A second reason that work is inherently satisfying is that every job makes a difference because every job serves a human need. Of course, there are jobs that make a *negative* difference—like drug trafficking. But every legitimate job is inherently satisfying because it provides some good or service that makes a difference to someone. One of our opportunities as individuals is to step back, and to see and acknowledge the difference that we make in our work. The main job of a supervisor is to show employees the difference their work makes. Because their work makes a difference, they make a difference.

Some jobs have evolved so that they don't make a difference any more. If the job doesn't make a difference, eliminate it. But work itself, all work, is inherently satisfying because it makes a difference: it serves a human need. I must add here that one person told me that he was making a good living and enjoying his work, but he had serious misgivings about it. He worked for a distributor of tobacco and firearms! He was seriously reconsidering whether he wanted to work for this company. It might be well to ask: What is the good or service I am providing in my current company? Perhaps many of us could create greater satisfaction by looking for new jobs that better align with our own values.

So work is not inherently dissatisfying; on the contrary, it is inherently satisfying because it allows us to do what we're good at, and it makes a difference for others. In upcoming chapters, I will take a closer look at how the work of individuals "lost in the corporation" makes a difference. I will also look more closely at the idea that the nature of work is that we can all do what we love to do and are good at. As a preview, if you are not good at what you are doing, get good. If you don't love what you are doing, do something else—or love what you are doing.

IS WORK IN THE UNITED STATES INHERENTLY DISSATISFYING?

Perhaps work in the *U.S.* is the problem—66% of *Americans* are dissatisfied. Yet, there is no reason to think that work in the United States is different than any other country. I might add here that when I conduct seminars in Canada and the U.K., I start my discussion about vacations by asking, "How many people took six or more weeks of vacation last year?" Of course, in the U.S. I would be laughed out of the room, so I start by saying "three weeks." Perhaps work in the U.S. is dissatisfying because we simply work too many hours. In that case, though, it is the number of hours we work that dissatisfies us, not the work itself. Other than how long we work, there is no reason to think work here is worse than any place else, and a lot of reasons to think it's better.

Dissatisfaction doesn't come from work itself, or from working in America. People are dissatisfied with work because of three things: 1) the way we interpret work, 2) the way we interpret satisfaction, and 3) the way we fail to take responsibility for creating satisfaction for ourselves. We have explored all of these concepts to some extent. In the upcoming chapters, I will further focus on taking responsibility for your own satisfaction.

Earlier, I said if you want your organization to be committed to excellence, *you* have to make that commitment first. We can carry it a step further. If the American system is not working, it's because we as individuals have not taken responsibility for creating satisfaction in our own lives. There is, in fact, no such thing as "the American System." There is simply: individuals performing jobs in America. It is one person and one person and one person creating satisfaction that reforms companies and industries and the whole country. Our commitment to our own satisfaction is the source, in fact, not only of American satisfaction but of global satisfaction.

AFFIRMATIONS

> ### The Nature of Work
>
> ❖ Work is inherently satisfying.
>
> ❖ My work serves others.
>
> ❖ I do what I love; I'm good at what I do.

CHAPTER 38

HOW TO CREATE SATISFACTION #1:
HAVE WHAT YOU CHOOSE OR
CHOOSE WHAT YOU HAVE

This is the first of seven ways to shift your thinking—or affirm your thinking if this is how you already see things—to create satisfaction in work and in life. These seven ways are not exclusive of each other, but are in fact interrelated to each other and to what was said previously. The last of the seven gives a practical action you can take to create satisfaction.

To begin with, one has to give up false independence in order to create satisfaction. In creating satisfaction we are not totally independent of the world around us. In fact, we are totally dependent. We live in an integral relationship with others and the entire planet. We cannot be truly satisfied when we are creating dissatisfaction in others. In society, then, seeking your satisfaction means that you let others know what you want and don't want, and they in turn let you know what they want and don't want. Our mutual satisfaction, then, comes about as a result of communication and often negotiation. Sometimes we get our way, sometimes they do, sometimes we both do and sometimes we compromise. Satisfaction is available in any of these cases.

Our satisfaction is linked not only to other people, but also to the rest of the universe. I would, in fact, be satisfied if my peach tree produced a fresh crop each month. However, I have dealt with the issue and have come to terms with the fact that it only produces once a year. I am now satisfied with that. I have made a compromise with the universe. That is, I realize that I live in relationship with the universe, and my satisfaction comes from cooperating with it, not resisting it. Our dance with the universe is: Sometimes I get what I want and sometimes I get what the universe wants. I have the option of being satisfied in either case. It comes from making peace with the universe.

A shorthand way of saying this is: Have what you choose or choose what you have. What does this mean? It means if you want something or want to change something, choose it—go for it: have what you choose. Or, if you can't change or achieve something, accept it: choose what you have. A variation of this principle is contained in the popular Serenity Prayer: "Lord, grant me the serenity to accept the things I can't change, the courage to change the things I can change and the wisdom to know the difference." Another variation of saying this is: Adjust reality to fit your expectations or adjust your expectations to fit reality. The most shorthand way of saying it is: Change it or choose it.

Dissatisfaction comes when reality doesn't fit your expectations. If you had no expectations—no wishes, desires, goals—then you would never be disappointed. However, since most of us have expectations, there are two ways to create satisfaction. First, go after what you expect or want—change things. Secondly, when you can't or won't or don't change reality, change your expectations—choose reality. Let's apply this to the workplace.

Most people who are dissatisfied are so because they haven't come to terms with what is dissatisfying them. They haven't asked themselves one or more of the following three questions:

1) What is it that I want that I think will create satisfaction for me?

2) What have I done to pursue this?

3) If I have attempted to achieve it and haven't succeeded, will I try again? If not, do I choose to accept the status quo?

How to Create Satisfaction

Let's look more closely at these three questions.

1) The first question involves people who are dissatisfied because they don't know what they want. More accurately, they think there is some preordained answer to what will satisfy them—the right job or right career —and they are waiting for the answer to manifest itself. Satisfied people are those who make a choice about what they think they want and then move forward to achieve it. If they find that this is not exactly what they want, they move forward to the next thing they think they want. Dissatisfied people, on the other hand, are waiting to be sure about what it is that they absolutely want, what will absolutely bring them satisfaction in life. This is clearly the way to condemn yourself to dissatisfaction. Satisfaction gets discovered in action. If you're not sure what it is that you want, don't worry about making the "right" choice; just pick something that you want and go for it.

To free ourselves to move forward, we need to create a win-win situation. Unfortunately, the scenario often looks like this instead: "If I go after a new career and don't like it, then I will lose. I am unsatisfied in my current career, so I am losing now." We place ourselves in lose-lose situations. To create a win-win situation we need to say, "I think I want to be in a new career/job, so I am going to go after it. If I enjoy it, I win. If I don't enjoy it, at least I will know that it is not for me. I will then be free to move on to something else." To have what you choose means to choose something and move toward having it.

Let's relate "having what you choose" to a spiritual point of view. Many people are concerned about finding out what God's will for them in life is: What is it that God wants me to do? It sometimes becomes an incapacitating thought; they cannot move forward because they are waiting. It's like waiting for Godot. Another way of looking at God's will is this: What God wants is for people to move forward with their lives. He wants us to create satisfaction in our life. He has no preconception about what he wants our lives to be. He in fact wants them to be whatever they are. And he has given us total freedom in creating our lives into what we want them to be. He has put the responsibility of choice on us. What we want or what we *think* we want is what's important to him. And it's okay with him if we make mistakes or change our mind or reach a goal and go on to another. On the other hand, we have absolutely no choice about being on a path. As long as you are alive you are on a path from birth to death. You had no choice in being on the path. What direction you go on the path, however, is entirely up to you. If you have what you choose you are having what God chooses. When you choose what you have the same is true. By the way, how do I know all this stuff about God? Read my next book entitled, *The 1-1/2 Minute Theologian*.

2) The second reason we may not be satisfied is reflected in the question: Have I pursued what I want? In this situation we have a pretty clear idea of what we want, but we just do not go after it. Why would a person not pursue what he says he wants? The answer is that there is a risk involved. In all decisions in life there is risk involved. There is a chance of losing something.

Let's look at the risk involved in dealing with four common causes of dissatisfaction in the workplace:

    A) Your relationship with your boss.
    B) Your relationship with subordinates.
    C) Overwork.
    D) Wanting to change jobs.

What is the risk involved with dealing with each of these situations?

    A) If you discuss what you want with your boss, he or she may get upset. You may get fired. The boss may see you negatively and impede your chances for promotion.

    B) If you are clear and forceful with your employees, they may quit, or they may resent you, or they may sabotage you.

    C) If you are overworked and deal with it, you will have to say no to your employer or to your clients or to your customers. The risk is, you may get fired or lose your clients or customers.

D) If you change jobs, you may be worse off than you are now. You may have to take a pay cut. You may have to move.

In all of these situations the downside we are risking may in fact occur. However, in the large majority of cases, what we feared doesn't occur, and we actually improve the situation. Even if the thing we wanted to avoid occurs, it may turn out to be a blessing in disguise. Many people who are fired are happier in their new jobs. When we don't move forward, fear is lurking beneath. This comes out of an attitude of scarcity, which I discussed earlier. On the other hand, people who pursue what they want create satisfaction— whether they get what they want or not. In summary, he first two reasons people are not satisfied are that we don't make a choice or we don't pursue the choice.

3) The third reason we may be dissatisfied relates to the question: Do I choose what I have? Much of our dissatisfaction comes from failure to accept or choose situations over which we have no control or over which we are not willing to exert control. For example, it would be appropriate for someone considering a job change to say: "I choose not to take the risk of looking for another job, so I am willing to stay in the job I have now. Since I am choosing to stay in this job and since there are things that I cannot control in this job, I choose to stop fighting them, to stop resenting them, to have it be okay for them be the way they are."

Likewise, you can apply the choose-what-I-have attitude to your relationship with your boss, peers, subordinates or clients: "I know I can't change their personalities, but I can change some behaviors. I push for what I want when it's important, and I don't sweat the little stuff. I choose it to be the way it is."

There is a difference between putting up with reality and choosing it. When we are putting up with reality we are resisting what's so. Resisting what's so never works. What works is changing what's so or accepting it. If we can't change what's so or we choose not to change it, the only other sensible option is to accept what's so. When you accept what's so, you say, "I cannot change this situation or I choose not to change it, so I am satisfied with it. I will not fight it or resist it, but I choose to have it be the way it is." This is not a cop-out but a true source of satisfaction. It's a choice to live in this world rather than some other world that we are creating in our mind. If you cannot have what you choose, the only other option is to choose what you have. This means to make that choice as a conscious act. There is a third option—go through life whining.

Choosing what you have applies to things even as difficult as approaching death. In fact, this is the ultimate choice that all of us have to make. Perhaps it is because people don't choose to accept their own mortality that they are not comfortable or not at peace with the world. When someone is terminally ill, how they may think about the illness will not alter the fact that they are going to die. Therefore, they have the option of leaving this world in a state of satisfaction or a state of dissatisfaction. They can leave the world either accepting what's so or resisting what's so. Satisfaction comes only from accepting what's so if it can't be changed.

But what if you decide to accept what's so because you can't or won't change it, and it keeps coming back to bother you, haunt you? For example, let's say you make the choice to accept your boss' irascible personality because you can't change it. But then you find that his/her actions continually bother you. If this happens, it's an indication that you probably *can* do something to change the situation. You are probably not taking the risk of confronting your boss by being assertive. Your lack of satisfaction implies that in the back of your mind is the thought, "This situation could be changed; my boss could act differently." That nagging thought is creating the dissatisfaction. If you were clear that your boss would not act differently, you wouldn't worry about it. The only way to eliminate the dissatisfaction is to try to change the situation. Personalities don't change but behavior does, and your forthrightness can influence your boss' behavior. When we truly accept the situation, truly choose what's so, a peaceful state follows. If you are not peaceful, that's an indication that you probably ought to act, to change the situation.

When you're stuck in limbo, neither willing to accept the situation nor willing to change it, there is some deeper source of your immobilization which needs to be uncovered. Perhaps what we're really reacting to in our boss, for example, is memories of the way our father treated us. We are not really reacting to the situation at hand, but we are adding something to it. And since we never expressed our emotions in the situation with our father, we are projecting them into this situation with our boss and are afraid to confront the boss. If you have situations in which you seem to be immobilized, you need professional help. Creating satisfaction may involve getting help though psychotherapy because you are subject to unfree, or addictive behaviors.

ADDICTIONS

Let's talk about addictive behavior, which ultimately is a great source of dissatisfaction. An addiction is the performance of an action where you are not free to do otherwise. For example, people who are addicted to drugs or alcohol or nicotine or over-eating are not free to simply stop. How can you tell whether you are addicted to something or not? The answer is very clear: Stop! If you can't, you are addicted. If you are a person who has smoked and you made a decision to stop, and you stopped and haven't smoked since, you are *not* addicted. If you made a decision to stop, if you made six or eight decisions to stop, and you still haven't, then you *are* addicted. So if you want to check whether you are addicted to drugs or alcohol or nicotine or over-eating, just stop doing any of them for a few weeks. If you find that you can't stop, or you live those few weeks longing for the day you can get back to it, you are clearly addicted.

Addictive behavior also happens on a psychological level. For example, some of us are addicted to always smiling and saying yes. Conversely, some are addicted to resisting authority: If somebody tells me to do something, I don't do it. In either case there is no freedom. If you consider yourself in the former category, just say no to the next three requests made of you. If you consider yourself in the second category, just say yes to the next three requests or orders given to you. If you can't do it, then clearly you are addicted.

Where do these addictive behaviors come from? In a very over-simplified way they go back to your childhood, probably your very early childhood, where your mother or father told you to do something and you decided to either capitulate or resist. It may not be quite as simple as that; then again, it may be. At any rate, addictions go back to our childhood and we need help to overcome them if we can't stop them.

The point is not necessarily to be free of all addictive drives but to recognize and control them. The drive may always be with you, but the control of it is in your power. People who are not free are those who say they are free and don't recognize that they have addictions. The first step in maturity is to recognize that you have patterned ways of acting or reacting over which you have little or no control. Once you recognize and admit it, then you can start to gain some control. A therapist, a Twelve- Step Program, or some outside source can help you recognize and control addictive behavior.

Creating satisfaction in all instances comes down to: Take responsibility for your satisfaction. *I* am the source of my satisfaction. The source of satisfaction is never outside of myself; it is always within. Another way of saying this is: If you are satisfied, *you* are creating the satisfaction, and if you are dissatisfied, *you* are creating the dissatisfaction. We are all capable of following this simple rule: Have what you choose or choose what you have.

AFFIRMATIONS

Choice

❖ I have what I choose and choose what I have.

❖ I change what I can and choose the rest.

❖ I live in harmony with the universe, whether acting or accepting.

❖ I live my life out of choice.

CHAPTER 39

HOW TO CREATE SATISFACTION #2: GIVE UP THE VICTIM MENTALITY

Another way of looking at failing to take responsibility for your satisfaction is to look at the distinction between being at the effect of your circumstances as opposed to being at cause or in control of them. People who are at the effect of their circumstances have a "victim mentality": My job causes my dissatisfaction; my boss causes my dissatisfaction; my salary causes my dissatisfaction; the weather causes my dissatisfaction; etc. They make their satisfaction dependent on external circumstances, and more often than not they are "victimized" by those circumstances.

There is a wonderful quote from George Bernard Shaw, and part of it gives a perfect statement of the victim mentality: "This is the true joy in life, the being used for a purpose recognized by yourself as a mighty one; the being a force of nature instead of a feverish, selfish little clod of ailments and grievances complaining that the world will not devote itself to making you happy." When we are in the "feverish, selfish little clod" mode, we say: Why wasn't I born into more money? Why didn't I have better parents? Why didn't I have better teachers? Why don't I have a good boss? A good job? And so on. This characterizes the victim mentality— being at the effect of or giving over control of your life to external circumstances.

Don't Go to Work Unless It's Fun!

The alternative to victim mentality is to be at cause or in control of your circumstances. What this means is that we are always free to either change our circumstances or to choose them. It is true that we do not cause our circumstances. What we do cause is our response to them. We can also cause ourselves to change the circumstances. If anything dissatisfies you in your work or in your life, either you can do something about it or you can't. The sooner you get clear about which it is, the sooner you create your own satisfaction.

Let's look at some ways that people put themselves at the effect of their circumstances:

- "There's always more work to do," as if I had no control over the amount of work I accept.
- "The job requires it," as if God designed my job and I have no say about it.
- "I have too many deadlines to meet," as if I didn't have any choice about agreeing to those deadlines or not.
- "My boss makes these demands on me," as if I can say nothing to my boss about how much or what kind of work I do.
- "It's the nature of the profession," as if God ordained that this is the way the profession should be.

If we translated these victim statements and took responsibility for being "at cause" in them, the statements would then look something like this:

- "I choose to accept more work than I can handle."
- "I overestimate what I can get done."
- "I am unrealistic in setting or accepting deadlines."
- "I don't say no to my boss or clients."
- "I accept too many responsibilities."
- "I agree to too much."

In all of these cases we place the responsibility squarely on our own shoulders. Once we do, we see that we have the option to change. Why don't we take responsibility for our circumstances?

It goes back to the attitude of scarcity: If I speak up I will lose my client or customer or job—and there is a scarcity of other jobs. The attitude is very similar to a slave mentality. A slave's livelihood is totally controlled by others. They have no options. But hasn't slavery been abolished?

Let's pursue this idea further: Even though legal slavery has been abolished, isn't it true that economic domination still takes place? Minorities and women are still, in fact, paid less than white males. Migrant workers and the poor are paid wages not adequate to live on. Perhaps it *is* legitimate to think of one's self as a victim. But let's take a closer look.

Let's presume that your situation was this: You are dissatisfied with your job, but you are raising a family and have settled in a certain area. You don't want to leave the area and don't want to give up your current salary. Already you've created three conditions. The job must be likeable, in this town, and at this salary. The reality is that you can have *any*thing you want but you can't have *every*thing you want. Maybe the job has to be different. Maybe the salary has to be different. Maybe the town has to be different. Where does satisfaction come from in this circumstance? It comes from looking at your options and choosing. Discuss moving with your family. Look at what salaries are available. Talk to people. Put out feelers. If you find that there's absolutely no other job where you can make the money you make now locally, then your only three options are: stay in this job, move, or work for a lower salary. In this world, those are the only options you have.

In the world of our imagination, we create another option: the job I like, at the salary I like, in the place I like. But, in the real world, satisfaction comes from exploring the real options, making a choice and rejoicing in it: "I rejoice that I am supporting my family, that we are living in the place where we're living and that I making the amount of money I am making. I am happy to be paying the necessary price to get what I want." This is not to say that you shouldn't try to achieve everything you want, but people who don't allow themselves to be victims look at their options realistically and make choices.

To carry this further, some slaves did, in fact, choose to be satisfied. They saw that they couldn't change their circumstances, or they chose not to try. So they created their own satisfaction within their circumstances. People in concentration camps did the same thing. Victor Frankl, in *Man's Search for Meaning*, wrote about the survivors in the concentration camps. They were people who created meaning in their lives within the circumstances in which they found themselves and over which they had no control. We have the same option: Live in the reality you live in, and have what you choose or choose what you have.

As I mentioned earlier, it takes either serenity or courage to stop living as a victim. It always takes courage to change. If it didn't take courage to change something, that something wouldn't be a problem for us. It wouldn't be a source of dissatisfaction. It is precisely because it is a source of dissatisfaction for us that it takes courage to change. Courage means there is a risk involved. We have something at risk, we may lose something.

The serenity of accepting the current situation is always an option. You don't have to take every risk presented to you. What is always called for, though, is to choose. Failure to choose is also a choice. It's a choice to accept the status-quo. However, when we don't consciously choose the status quo, no satisfaction comes with it because it is a choice by default. Satisfaction only comes from taking the risk of changing or from making a conscious decision to accept the current situation. When we don't make clear choices and opt for victimhood instead, we pay the price of on-going dissatisfaction.

DO WHAT YOU LOVE; THE MONEY WILL FOLLOW

In this discussion about choices, I implied that there is no such thing as "the perfect job." Let me back off from that. There is a book entitled *Do What You Love; The Money Will Follow* by Marsha Sinetar. The point of the book is exactly what the title says: Don't worry about money, just do what you love to do and the money will come. Although the content of the book was not personally useful to me, I was excited by the title every time I picked it up. I believe that the title is true; it is "the better way." This ties in with the nature of work which I spoke of earlier: Work is everybody doing what they love to do and what they are good at.

At some seminars I ask, "If you won the lottery, who would be doing pretty much what you're doing now a year from now?" One third of the people raise their hands. Were they blessed by divine decree? No, they are people who take responsibility for their own satisfaction. I ask myself a similar question: If I were to retire what kind of life would I be leading? The answer is that I would be leading pretty much the same kind of life I am leading now. I would work. I love to create and teach seminars. I love to write books. I love to make audio-tapes. I also love the fact that I am making money from doing these things and am able to support my family. So I consider myself one of the people who is doing what he loves and the money is following. Everyone can be in this position, given that they pay their dues.

What does paying your dues mean? It means one of two things: have what you choose or choose what you have. For me to get into the position I am in, I had to make certain choices which involved risk. I had to start my own business. I had to create seminars. I had to sell them. I had to present them to see how they went over. I had to pursue new ideas and sell them and present them. These are some of the risks I took which got me to where I am. On the other hand, there are certain areas about "doing what I love" in which I choose what I have. For example, I don't particularly enjoy the traveling aspect of my work. I enjoy it generally, but when I get into my "busy season" I miss my family and find the travel physically stressful. However, that goes with the current territory of this job. I am working on ways that I can do more, earn more and travel less; hopefully they will come along. But, for the time being, I choose what I have and I love what I do.

If you're not doing what you love right now, I suggest you love what you do. When I graduated from college, I became an English teacher and taught high school English for five years. After that, I took an administrative job in a continuing education organization. I used to tell people, "I'm just doing this until I decide what I want to do." After three years in the job, I recognized that I was no closer to knowing what I wanted to do than the day I started. So I made a decision: I pretended that this was what I wanted to do, what I wanted to be when I grew up. That decision made a significant difference. I started taking more responsibility in the job. I became more proactive. I grew in the work. I got a promotion. Eventually

I grew out of the work to starting my own business.

If you are clear about what you love and you are not pursuing it now, pursue it. If you're not clear about what you love, love what you do. There was a popular country and western song a while ago, "Take This Job and Shove It." This is the perfect embodiment of victim mentality. I am also told that someone has audio-tapes entitled, "Take This Job and Love It." Much more preferable, much more responsible. Victimhood doesn't do anybody any good. It is the way we create dissatisfaction.

AFFIRMATIONS

> **Giving Up a Victim Mentality and Taking Responsibility**
>
> ❖ I am at cause in my life.
>
> ❖ I create the universe I desire.
>
> ❖ I love my work.
>
> ❖ I grow in doing what I love to do every day.

CHAPTER 40

HOW TO CREATE SATISFACTION #3: MAKING A DIFFERENCE VERSUS MAKING A LIVING

Satisfaction comes from being able to make this simple statement: I make a difference. When people know they make a difference in the world, they are satisfied. When people don't think they make a difference, they are dissatisfied. Let's analyze this proposition more closely.

How do you know that you make a difference? In the world of work there are three conditions. These are based on the premise I discussed earlier that work is inherently satisfying because it provides goods and services that fulfill human needs. The three conditions for making a difference are:

1) I contribute to my team.
2) The team produces results.
3) The results make a difference.

Let's look at each of these separately.

1) I CONTRIBUTE TO MY TEAM

Whomever you work with is your team. To get a clear sense of your role on that team ask: If I didn't do this job, what would happen? One possible answer might be: "If I didn't do this job somebody else would. Therefore, I don't make a difference." People use this reasoning to invalidate the contribution they actually make. The fact that you are "replaceable" doesn't mean that what you're doing doesn't make a difference. The fact that someone else could do it is beside the point. As long as you are doing it, you are the someone who is producing the results. You are a positive link in the chain of production. You clearly have a contributing role on the team.

Of course, as human beings we want to keep growing and sometimes become dissatisfied with doing something that someone else could do. This is fine, because it may lead us to do something that no one else could do. It may lead us to making a unique contribution that no one else is making or even *could* make. This is the higher level of fulfillment which Maslow speaks of as "self-actualization." But even if what we are contributing to the team is not unique, it still is of value. It does make a contribution to what the team is producing.

One of the drawbacks of industrialized society is that jobs are broken down into such minute areas of responsibility that people lose sight of the whole that they are producing: "I attach this portion to the micro-chip we're producing; I handle accounts payable for this department; I pick the baby's breath." (Note: I will build on these three examples in the rest of this chapter.) We don't see the overall difference that our little part plays in the whole. As workers, we need to acknowledge that we are making a contribution and to acknowledge our co-workers' contribution. This may be the most important role of a manager.

I make a difference because I play a role on the team, and the team makes a difference because what we produce makes a difference. Every job on the team is important. Every job does make a difference. If it doesn't, get rid of it. Don't stay in a job that doesn't make a difference, and don't keep people in jobs that don't make a difference.

Let's compare your work team to the human body. Is every part of your body important? The answer is obviously, yes. This is a different question from: Is every part of your body essential? Is your baby toe essential? The answer is, no. Is your baby toe important? The answer is, yes. If it's not important, get rid of it.

How about your baby toenail? Even that's important. If it's not, get rid of it. So all parts of the human body are important. Yet, there are relative degrees of importance to our parts. Can we say what's most important? Most people probably would say the brain. What is second most important? Probably the heart. Where would you rate the large intestine in this hierarchy? It doesn't matter. Your large intestine is not only important, but essential. So some parts of the body are essential; all parts are important. So, too, all workers in an organization must see clearly that the job that they are doing is important. It makes a contribution; it makes a difference. It may not be essential, but it's important. Otherwise it wouldn't be there. You do have a role on the team. You contribute to the team. When you acknowledge this, you shift your attitude from merely making a living to making a difference.

Then there are those who have the attitude, "I was really meant for better things than this job." If you were meant for better things, go after them. If you choose not to go after them, celebrate what you are doing. In the movie "Coming To America," Eddie Murphy, an African prince, gets a job in a hamburger restaurant in the U.S. He proudly says: "I am in charge of garbage. Do you have any today?" He was proud of what he did. He didn't let his "status" of prince negate the fact that he was making a difference. Collecting garbage makes a difference. You can do it with two attitudes: "This is my job. I'm proud of what I do. I do a good job. It makes a difference." Or you can say, "This is a lousy job. It is beneath me. I was made for better things." The second attitude is the victim attitude. The former attitude is the one that will carry someone forward to actually do "better things."

Whatever job you're doing, you make a contribution to your team. You make a difference. Acknowledge it, affirm it, celebrate it. If you are meant for better things, go after them.

One other way of looking at the difference you make to your team—if you choose to make a difference—is the way you interact with them daily. That is, you can choose to make a positive contribution to every one you work with each day. This applies to the clients, customers, other people you deal with as well. Whether you are producing Hartz collars or performing heart surgery, you can choose to make a contribution to the people with whom you come in contact. There are many contributions you can make, but the fundamental one is: Do you *listen* to people? Do you actually allow yourself to be interested in other people, to be open to them? This is a difference you can make to everybody every day. However, as I said earlier, it's not that you give up your own satisfaction in order to try to secure it for others. You primarily take responsibility for your own needs. And, while doing this, you can be conscious of serving the needs of others. In this way you can make a difference at work every day.

2) THE TEAM PRODUCES RESULTS

Each individual member of the work team makes a difference because the team itself produces results: "We are producing our quota of micro chips that work. We are receiving and processing payment for bills. We are getting all of our flowers picked, packaged and to market in good shape." One of the best ways to show people that they make a difference is to show the overall results your department/company produces. Let them know that the team is producing results: "You were part of the effort that produced micro chips for 50,000 computers this year. You were part of a team that made sure that the $10 million we paid out this year was accurate. You were part of the team that got 60,000 bouquets into people's houses this year."

I might add here that a potent way to give people pride in the accomplishment of their team is profit-sharing. If I have a financial reward added to the sense of accomplishment I get from my work, then that is even further incentive to produce results. People should not only take pride in the results that the team produces, but they should also share in the financial rewards. Everyone loves a piece of the action. This will ultimately create bigger pies so that everyone wins—owners, workers and the clients or customers they serve.

It is important to measure and talk about results. When the results are positive, we can see and acknowledge the difference we're making. When they're poor, we can ask why and make the necessary changes.

3) THE RESULTS MAKE A DIFFERENCE

If our team, department, division, company is producing results, the next question to ask is: Do the results make a difference? The answer is: Yes. All companies do make a difference, otherwise they wouldn't be in existence. Following up on the three examples I used earlier, each of those companies make a difference to me personally: I am delighted I have a computer; it makes my work much easier. I am delighted that companies which provide me with goods and services have good records and keep track of how much money comes in and how much money goes out—including how much I owe them—so that they can stay in existence. I am delighted that I can buy flowers at the supermarket to beautify my home. The goods or services companies provide make a difference. They serve people. We lose sight of that. We need to get back in touch with the fact that every job serves a human need.

There is a hierarchy of human needs. Jobs that produce food are more important than those that produce skateboards. Skateboards are more important than cigarettes. I spoke earlier of the person who worked for a distributor of tobacco and firearms. He had a real moral dilemma, and I would too. There are perhaps positive values to tobacco and firearms. But what if everybody who worked in those industries said: "I am making more of a negative difference than a positive difference. I am going to quit and find a job that makes a greater, more positive contribution to people." If everybody did that, there would be no more cigarettes or guns! People, of course, don't do that because they don't see or don't look for alternatives. They then sink back to the level of making a living rather than making a difference. I am not faulting them, but when people really are concerned about the morality of what they are producing, they create an alternative.

People who see themselves as making a living instead of making a difference shift much of their energy into protecting their jobs rather than in looking at how they could make a greater difference. I heard of one company president who said, "If you can show me how to eliminate your job, I'll guarantee you a job for life." What a joy to be working to make a difference rather than to protect your turf! If you are working for an organization that doesn't make as great a difference as you would like, it takes courage to try to change it. Perhaps it's time to look for a new organization, or to create your own.

What would happen if everyone left organizations for ones in which they felt they made a greater difference, a greater contribution? We would have a profound groundswell of new, positive, dynamic, contributing organizations.

People who operate out of the concept of scarcity—that there aren't enough jobs, there isn't enough money, there aren't enough resources—do not have a very useful picture of the world. Here is a more useful way of viewing it: There are plenty of jobs around, in fact, millions. If we look at job formation not from the viewpoint of what exists now, but from the viewpoint of what human needs are not being met, we create a whole new interpretation of work and job formation. Every job springs from a human need. There are plenty of needs around, so there are plenty of potential jobs around. We just have to look. For example, look at how many homeless and hungry people there are in our country. People need houses, training, counselling, rehabilitation, day-care, capital. There are a multitude of unanswered needs in this country and therefore a multitude of potential jobs. We simply have to create the jobs. The reason we don't is that people are still tied to making a living instead of making a difference. And this attitude goes all the way up to the top levels in government which create (or fail to create) policy on jobs.

I suggest that organizations not only acknowledge what it is they produce, but that they celebrate it. Every organization should have a mission statement. The word origin of "mission" is: "Something we were sent to do." It implies something special, something important, something that makes a difference for people. In contrast, an objective of an organization simply says: Here's what we're trying to do. A mission statement is an objective with a vision behind it: Here is the difference that we're trying to make. Here is what we are creating that will produce meaningful results in the world. A mission statement answers the question: What do we stand for?

The purpose of a mission statement is not to have some words we can write on a brochure, but to have something that makes us want to get up and go to work in the morning: "What I am doing is to create the spread of as much information to as many people as possible. What I am doing is assuring that people who have contributed goods and services to our company are paid fairly and quickly. What I am doing is bringing the beauty of nature into people's homes." Even if your organization doesn't have a mission statement, I suggest that you create your own private mission statement for your organization, one that will give meaning to your work. Perhaps you can be the leaven to create a mission statement for your organization.

The current mission statement of Frank Sanitate Associates is to transform people's relation to work so that they work smarter, produce more and, best of all, look forward to going to work every day. Our goals are to make a contribution, make a profit, and have fun!

Everyone wants to make a contribution. It is that desire which is the source of so much volunteer work in America. People serve their churches, their communities, and charitable organizations often with more fervor, intelligence and energy than they serve their regular job, because they see the difference that it makes. What would it take for people to have that same fervor in their paid work?

When an organization commits to higher purposes, to making a difference in people's lives, it engages the higher energies of those who work for it. If you seem to be buried in the depths of an organization and you aren't clear about the difference you're making, go and ask your boss. If you're not enamored with the contribution your organization is making and you choose not to go to another one, at least acknowledge that your organization is making *some* contribution to people. You can still have as a personal objective to make a contribution every day —not only the contribution you make to society, but also the one you make to co-workers and the people with whom you come in contact. Treating everyone as if they made a difference is the biggest difference you can make.

In summary, people create satisfaction when they make a difference instead of just making a living. They make a difference when they have a clear sense of their contribution to the team, the team produces results, and the results make a difference.

AFFIRMATIONS

> ### Making a Difference
>
> ❖ I make a difference.
>
> ❖ My work makes a difference.
>
> ❖ I go to work every morning to contribute to people's lives.

CHAPTER 41

HOW TO CREATE SATISFACTION #4: LIVE IN THE QUESTION

The problem and also opportunity of asking the question, "What creates satisfaction?" is that there is no single answer. The answer seems to constantly shift. As evidenced in this book, there are many answers. Perhaps the solution is to give up the idea that there is an answer and to acknowledge that what satisfies us shifts. This allows us to "live in the question," to continually be open to what we need to do to create satisfaction in the moment. It is an ongoing inquiry which gives us the freedom to create our life anew every day—in fact, at every moment.

As I said earlier, in discussing Herzberg's Hygiene/Motivation theory, we can interpret the question, "What will satisfy me?" in two ways: The first is from the viewpoint of dissatisfaction—is there anything that is dissatisfying me right now? The second is from a neutral state—nothing is dissatisfying me right now, but what will it take to satisfy me? Making this distinction makes it a lot easier to live in the question: What will satisfy me? The answer to the "hygiene" part of the question is: I handle, resolve all those things that dissatisfy me. I spoke about overcoming the victim mentality. If we take a stand to handle those things that dissatisfy us, then we will never be at the mercy of our circumstances. In other words, don't carry around any negatives, any dissatisfiers. Clear them out whenever you become aware of them.

Concerning the "motivation" part of the question, if you're honest with yourself you'll recognize that there have been times when you achieved what you had been striving for, but it did not really bring satisfaction. We say: If I had a new boss, this job would be satisfying; if I had a new job then I would be satisfied; if I made just $20,000 more; if I had this house; if I just had this car, and so on.

Even in our relationships we play this game: If I could just meet the right man or the right woman; if my mom, my spouse, my child just stopped doing this, etc. After we actually get what we say we want and we see we're not satisfied by it, we sometimes pretend that we didn't really know what we wanted then—but we do now: "I thought I really wanted a Cadillac, but I didn't. What I really want is a Mercedes." Or, "I thought I'd be satisfied when I graduated from college, but now I need to get a better job to be satisfied." We get the job and then we say, "Well, I thought this job would satisfy me, but I really need to be in a higher paying position." And so on.

We affirm our present decisions but negate our past decisions. A much healthier way of operating would be to affirm both the past and present decisions: "I was exploring what I wanted then, and I'm exploring it now. I wasn't sure then, but I moved forward to where I am now. I'm not sure exactly where I want to go now, but this is the direction I'm moving in." That is what it means to "live in the question."

Living in the question reaffirms what I talked about under "The Seven Scarcities." We start from the viewpoint: I am not lacking anything now; nothing is wrong now *and* I want more. For example, if you own a Ford and would like to own a Mercedes, an accurate way to describe the situation is: "It's not bad that I have a Ford; in fact, it's good. I'm happy that I have a Ford rather than nothing, *and* I would like a Mercedes." It's not that we are dissatisfied, but that we are satisfied, *and* we're looking for even greater satisfaction. Living in the question of what creates satisfaction means: "Not only do I handle those things that dissatisfy me, but I also affirm my satisfaction. I am satisfied now and I look forward to creating greater satisfaction for myself. What's next for me?"

Is it possible to extend this thinking to get rid of dissatisfiers altogether? For example, could we say: "My Ford is not running and it needs to be fixed. I am delighted that I have a Ford that needs to be fixed." From this point of view, it's not a problem that the car isn't running but really an opportunity. It comes from the attitude: Things are good and this needs to be handled, rather than, things are bad and this needs to be handled.

This can even be applied to physical pain: "I am delighted that I have a toothache. I don't like the ache, but I'm happy I have the tooth. Now, how do I take care of the ache?" At first, this might seem naive. But in the broader picture, what is really naive is to suffer—to complain, to feel sorry for yourself, to feel that this shouldn't happen to you. I make the distinction here between "pain" and "suffering." Pain is very real and undesirable. Suffering is the attitude we take toward pain—and sometimes the attitude we take when pain isn't even present. It's becoming a "victim" to the pain. With either attitude, victim or not, the facts are the same: You have a tooth, it aches, you need to take care of it. You are free to choose the attitude you take toward the facts. Pain may be inevitable, but suffering is *optional.* It makes more sense to have a positive attitude and ask what's next rather than to suffer and ask what's next, or just suffer without even asking what's next!

An analogy: When a stream flows down a mountain and comes to a big rock right in the middle of its path, it doesn't get upset. It doesn't get annoyed, frustrated, depressed, fearful. It just does what comes next. Maybe it goes around the rock; maybe it rises until it goes over the rock; maybe it finds a hole and goes underground. Water doesn't care. It dances with the universe. It wisely allows the universe to lead.

So, living in the question means that we voluntarily dance with the universe. We happily ask: What's next? We declare our satisfaction now, and we are open to what's next.

AFFIRMATIONS

> ### Living in the Question
>
> ❖ I am whole, total and complete now, and I'm open to what's next.
>
> ❖ I am totally satisfied now, and I continue to grow more satisfied.

CHAPTER 42

HOW TO CREATE SATISFACTION #5: LIVE IN TENSION —LIVE IN BALANCE

One way of summarizing several of the concepts I have discussed in this book is to look at the paradox of tension: One must live without tension to be satisfied and one must live in tension to be satisfied. Let's look at the first kind of tension.

The kind of tension we all can and should do without is living in a state of stress, anxiety or pressure. As I discussed earlier, these states all come from within, from the way we interpret the world around us. Our actions flow out of the interpretations. Many of us have deeply ingrained attitudes or interpretations about reality that come from our early childhood. These are the sources of tension. Unless you've been through therapy or counseling or very special communications with family or friends, it's hard to see the mental traps in which you may have put yourself. For example, a trap that I lived in for a long time was the rule: Be nice and don't upset anybody. This was a very ingrained rule which I didn't even realize I lived by until well into my adulthood. The tension that "being nice" created was that I often said yes when I wasn't quite sure if I wanted to say yes. This was an unhealthy tension, not the kind of tension I needed to live with.

Maturity or freedom comes when we recognize the ingrained rules, habits or pictures that we have been living out of without choice, and then freely choose to follow those rules or not. This is what I discussed in talking about addictions. It is very helpful for me to be able to realize that on the one hand I am addicted to being nice and saying yes, and on the other I don't always want to say yes. Then I can consider whether I want to say yes in this case or not. Bringing unconscious choices into consciousness helps to resolve much of that harmful tension which results in stress and anxiety. We are then at a point where we can make free decisions.

On the other hand, there is a second tension, a good tension which we must live with in order to create satisfaction. That tension is better defined as balance. Tension implies two poles, with one or the other eventually winning. Balance implies two values with *both* winning, each in their time, or both simultaneously. In other words, it means that you don't give one up for the sake of the other; you create a way of achieving both. "Either/or" thinking is often valuable in decision-making: There are two paths; take one or the other. But "either/or" thinking is not valuable when "both/and" thinking is called for—thinking that doesn't negate one of the two values but encompasses them both in balance.

Many times management and personal growth seminars focus on rules: Always do this. This thinking may polarize us. Pursuing one value may lead to excluding another value. For example, I hear of many companies that have an "open door/answer your own phone" policy. There is a value in this policy, that of availability. Yet there is also a value in blocking out periods of time for yourself when you can work without interruption. Both availability and solitude are values. We need to create a balance to achieve both, not a tension where one gets sacrificed for the other.

THE TEN BALANCES

We need ten balances. They each represent two values, both of which need to be pursued. They are the balance between:

1. Your work life and your personal life: I discussed this extensively in the section on overwork. You need to put in enough
   hours to do your job well, and you need to be home enough for
   a satisfactory personal life.

2. Doing and managing: Most people have two components in their job, doing and managing. The "doing" part of your job is the technical work that you do. The four functions of management are: planning, organizing, directing and evaluating. You need to take away time from the doing part of your job in order to manage your job (plan, organize, evaluate) and manage others (direct). So your real job is to balance the doing and managing parts of your job.

3. Daily recurring activities and tasks/projects: There are certain daily recurring activities that are part of our job, but we often don't consider them to be part of our job—managing, handling mail, returning calls, handling interruptions, professional reading, administrative tasks. What we normally call "work" are the tasks and projects we do. Yet both are aspects of our work and we need to balance both.

4. Being available and getting our planned work done: This is the example I spoke of earlier. Interruptions are part of our job. We need to be available to our clients or customers, our boss, our co-workers, our staff. Yet constant interruptions prevent us from getting our planned work done. So we also need blocks of time for our planned work when we are not available to anyone. We need to balance availability with getting our planned work done. There are two ways to serve your clients: by talking to them, and by *not* talking to them and getting their work done.

5. Growth and consolidation: Much of the stress encountered in business comes from rapid growth. The old patterns are not adequate to handle the new volume, so change is constant. In a changing world, if you are not growing, you are declining. Yet, businesses and people need to take time to consolidate their growth, to catch their breath, to catch up and get reorganized. Businesses ought to say "No" to growth sometimes so that people and the organization don't get worn thin. Many businesses have a busy season and a slack season. The slack season is the best time for consolidation, reorganization. All

busy-ness is not healthy; neither is all slack. Companies need to balance growth and consolidation.

6.   Billable and non-billable time: Those who bill out their time— lawyers, CPAs, engineers, etc.—often refer to their billable hours as "productivity." The fallacy in this label is that it is often *more* productive to be doing things that are *not* billable— planning, supervising others, training others and yourself. If you don't take time to work smarter, you generally work harder. Billable hours are what put bread on the table, but the non-billable often secure us more abundant future bread. There must be a balance between billable and non-billable hours to do your total job.

7.   Short-term and long-term goals: This is the balance between handling daily problems, emergencies, exigencies (the reactive part of our job) and setting long term goals (the proactive part of our job). Many times we get consumed by the "tyranny of the urgent" and forget about the long term goals that we set, if indeed we set them! Balance means taking care of both short-term needs and long-term goals.

8.   Results and process: This balance, which I discussed earlier, is the balance between goals and process, between getting satisfaction from the goals achieved and from the process of achieving itself. In business, as in life, we are so intent on "getting *there*," on producing the end result, that we often forget that the "*getting* there" is where we're spending our lives. If we aren't enjoying the process, we are missing the boat. Yet, we have to produce results as well. Balance means we enjoy both the achieving and achievements.

9.   Serving others and serving ourselves: Although I discussed this previously, let's take a deeper look. Do we not have an obligation or responsibility to serve others as well as ourselves? Of course, but the word "obligation" contains the idea of "have to/should/must" within it. What if we translated this negative interpretation ("obligation") into a positive

one? How about: "We have the privilege of serving others." It is a privilege to be a parent. It is a privilege to be able to serve others in our work.

But what about when it doesn't feel like a privilege, when it starts to feel like an obligation, a "should"? Where is the point of balance between serving others and serving ourselves? The key to answering that question is to ask: When does serving others start to create dissatisfaction for me? Ideally, serving others is the same as serving ourselves. When we serve others we get satisfaction from it. When we stop getting satisfaction, then it's time to shift: Either change it (stop serving, at least in this way) or choose it (get back to *why* you are serving and see if you still want to do it).

People who are "givers" often get burned out. When serving others shifts from a want to into a have to, it is no longer serving others. If you *have* to love someone, you don't really love them. If parents resentfully stay in a marriage only for "the sake of the children," they are not doing their children any favors. One needs to have the courage to monitor one's own satisfaction. Those who are trapped in the give-till-it-hurts syndrome may have to go cold turkey: Just say no. Get back to taking care of yourself for a while so you can create a better balance in serving both others and yourself.

10. The last balance is the balance between doing and not doing: We need to have both active and reflective parts to our lives.

In speaking about "not doing", I want to talk specifically about the four "Re's" which my old novice master talked about when I had first joined a religious order: recreation, relaxation, repose, and refection. The point which he made about them is that none of them is an end or goal in itself. They are means to an end. Let's look at them individually. The prefix "re," by the way, means "back" or "again."

- Recreation: The purpose of recreation or play is really to re-create ourselves. It is to create or renew ourselves once again. It is a pulling back so we can then go forward.

- Relaxation: Relaxation comes from the latin words "re" and "laxare," meaning "to loosen again." When you relax, you are loosening up what has become tight or tense. Once you are loose, you are able to move forward again.

- Repose: This comes from "re" and "pausare," meaning "to stop again." Possibly it goes further back to the verb, "posui," which means "to place or put." So when you are reposing or sleeping, you are pausing, putting yourself back into place, repositioning yourself.

- Refection: This is not a common word. The word refectory may be a little more familiar, a place where you eat. Refection means taking refreshment, nourishment - eating and drinking. (Notice the word "refreshment"!) Refection comes from the latin words "re" and "facere," which means "to make or do again." So, when we are eating, we are making ourselves over again or restoring ourselves. (Notice the word "restore.")

The point that my novice master made about the four "re's" is that they are all temporary, all states of pausing in order to move forward again. Once you are created again, once you are loosened again, once you are placed again, once you are made again—what is there to do except to move forward? None of these activities is a goal in itself. They are just means of pulling back so that we can go forward.

My novice master had a valid point concerning these activities. He also had an anti-pleasure streak in him. He felt that these activities were to be tolerated, at best. However, we ought to look at them positively as well. We ought to look forward to play and rest and food and to enjoy them when we are partaking. They are valuable and wonderful to do for their own sake. But, when we are playing or resting or eating too much, they then become negative activities. But what is "too much"? How do we define what is too much and what isn't?

If we find these activities satisfying, then they are good. They are good up to the point where they become dissatisfying to us. Once we are full, to continue eating creates dissatisfaction. If we are rested, but continue to stay in bed, we become "restless." Even too much recreation, or play, can become dissatisfying. A child can be content in building a sand castle, but as he grows he wants to begin to build a *real* castle, something that is useful. Otherwise, he has a life of washed-away castles, which is not satisfying. So we begin to train ourselves to forego what might be a short-term gratification for the sake of long-term gratification.

I have been speaking of "not doing" as the four "Re's." We can also look at a higher aspect of not doing—contemplation. Some theologies see this as the highest value in life. Indeed, they see the after-life as "the beatific vision," the perpetual contemplation of the beauty of God. Whatever happens after we die, in *this* life contemplation is nice work if you can get it. All of us need quiet times, times of being, times of contemplation. Very few of us are accustomed to taking them. However, if we spent all of our time contemplating the beauty of the earth, there are two problems: 1) These times may become boring or unsatisfying, and 2) We may neglect the practical necessities of life.

All of the pleasures of life including contemplation and the four "Re's"—all of the "not doing" times—are valuable. So is the doing. Life is maximized when we balance both.

In conclusion, we achieve balance by making conscious decisions in all ten areas of balance. The rule in life is that there are no rules in life. We have the opportunity of living moment-by-moment and creating balance. The rudder that guides us through life is our own sense of satisfaction at each given moment.

AFFIRMATIONS

Living in Balance

❖ I have everything in life in balance.

❖ I serve others and serve myself.

❖ I choose to play; I choose to work.

CHAPTER 43

HOW TO CREATE SATISFACTION #6: BALANCE THE THREE "C'S"

When I look at all of the facets of my work, and of work in general, I see that satisfaction does not come from just one thing, but from three things. In the last chapter I spoke of keeping a balance in order to create satisfaction. In this chapter I want to discuss another type of balance from which we get satisfaction, a balance among the three "C's": Creation, Completion and Control. Satisfaction comes from each of these three C's in their time. Sometimes satisfaction comes from creating things, at other times from completing things, and at other times from controlling or putting order to things. Overall satisfaction comes from achieving a balance among all three C's. When we take one of the C's and try to make that the sole source for satisfaction, it ultimately creates dissatisfaction. Let's take a closer look at each of the three C's.

The first C is Creation. In order to create satisfaction, human beings need to create—to produce something new. Otherwise, we are cogs in machines other people have created. However, there are people who stress creativity to the detriment of control and completion. We characterize them as the "creative types." They are constantly coming up with new ideas, new schemes to work on. The excitement of the creative act carries them forward until the next new creative idea comes up, and then they pursue that idea because there is more energy and excitement in it. They are constantly creating but seldom completing.

When we operate only in this mode, we ultimately create dissatisfaction—that is, unless we have a patron who is financially supporting us while we play our creative games. Even if we did have a patron, we still wouldn't be satisfied ultimately because we would look behind us and see a trail of broken dreams—ideas that we started but never completed.

The next C is Completion. I spoke earlier of incompletion as one of the main sources of dissatisfaction. The opposite is wonderful— to complete things. We all know the joy of having 13 tasks on our list and crossing off every one, or of pushing forward on a project and finally completing it. In this mode we are completing one thing after another, doing one task, seeing it through to completion and then taking on the next task.

Yet, we can get trapped in this C as well, to the detriment of the other two. If our whole life is consumed in simply performing one task after another, we are ultimately not satisfied. It is as if we were cogs in a machine, pushing out one result after the other. We are not in charge of completion; completion takes charge of us and we become its slave. In this mode, we are pursuing control to some degree since we have to control our environment to complete tasks. However, we are not in control of our overall well-being. On the contrary, circumstances are controlling us. And we are missing the spark of creativity that gives purpose and juice to the tasks or projects we're working on.

The third C is Control. Control, order, organization are required to bring anything to completion. There can be great satisfaction in putting order to things. Control is what gives us the ability to order our environment rather than be ordered by it. However, we can get caught up in the process of controlling to the detriment of either creation or completion. We can spend our whole day and our whole life having an orderly in-box, an orderly desk, an orderly office, an orderly house, an orderly work-space. We can put an inordinate amount of time in being orderly about things. We can spend the whole day planning without ever completing any of our plans. We lose sight of the fact that creating order is only a means and not an end in itself.

I take that back. Creating order, controlling, can be fun and satisfying in itself. But it doesn't produce anything. So unless you have that patron to support you, you can't give your life over to control. The purpose of creating order is so that we can complete things, carry things to fruition—which then gives us the space or opportunity to be creative again. We need the space or leisure or freedom to allow creative thoughts to come, and we need to pursue and complete those creations. Control permits both of these.

So creating satisfaction means to balance all three C's—Creation, Control, and Completion—by giving the appropriate amount of time to each. How does one do that? Several of the ideas I have shared in Section Four deal with how to get control of your time and how to complete things. Below are some ideas on how to achieve and balance all three C's, especially creativity.

CREATION: HOW TO ENHANCE YOUR CREATIVITY
Concerning creativity, you probably can identify yourself in one of three categories:

1) Yes, I am a creative person, but I just don't have time to give to my creativity.
2) No, I am not very creative and would like to learn how to be creative.
3) Yes, I am creative, and I take the time I want to create.

Most people seem to classify themselves in the first category. If you do, you need to give yourself permission to be creative at times when creative thoughts occur to you. For example, if you are in the middle of a task or project and an extraneous creative idea comes to you, stop and take the time to develop that idea immediately—or finish the immediate task and then give yourself time to develop the idea.

If you are lying in bed at night and great thoughts are running through your head, get up and write them down or dictate them. What if you are so brilliant that you are up from 1:00 to 4:00 in the morning dictating these great ideas? Have your spouse call the office the next day and tell them you'll be in at noon because you were working late last night. If you don't have that option and have to drag yourself into work, it's a small price to pay for what you've produced the previous night. When the creative muse hits us, those times can produce ten or one hundred times the benefit that keeping your nose to the grindstone will produce. If you let that moment go by, it may never return; the grindstone, however, is always there for you. Give in to creative impulses periodically.

How can you quantify or measure whether you're giving yourself enough time for creativity? Set a weekly goal for yourself: "I will spend at lease three hours this week in creative work/play." Check up on yourself next week to see whether you did claim those periods of creativity for yourself when they occurred. If you didn't, actually schedule some time for yourself this week for creativity, a time for just doing nothing and seeing where your mind takes you.

What if you are in the second category, someone who doesn't consider yourself particularly creative? How do you become creative—just schedule a time to be creative, and hope for the best? Yes, if that's all you can think of doing. It's better than doing nothing about creativity. However, there are two ways to enhance your creativity:

1) Create space, and
2) Prime the pump.

What do these mean?

1) CREATE SPACE

Creating space means to put yourself in an atmosphere or environment where you are more likely to generate ideas. Generally that means away from noise and distractions. It means to put yourself where you actually feel free, safe and unreachable. It might be in your back yard, or in a library, or in your bedroom or on the beach. When you are in this safe space, get comfortable and allow yourself to just *be*. Stop trying to think about things. What happens when you stop trying to think about things? Answer: You think about things! But it's a different mode of thinking. It is shifting from left to right brain thinking. In other words, you're not trying to resolve things, to figure out things, to think things through. Trying is a left brain activity. Creative thinking is a right brain activity. It is passive. You allow your right brain to operate by sitting back and seeing what ideas float through your mind freely and spontaneously without necessarily trying to control them. We have a constant stream of thoughts flowing through our mind, and creating space allows us to see them. It's like sitting back and watching the movies in your mind. While you're in this daydreaming phase, have a tape recorder or paper and pencil handy to record ideas that come up.

If you are not the kind of person who allows yourself to pursue creative thoughts when you have them, this is the only thing that will work. If you try this a few times—give yourself a good period of time, at least one hour—and find that you get no creative ideas, then I invite you to create a better way to be creative. Creative ideas, by the way, are not necessarily grandiose like designing buildings, composing symphonies, becoming the greatest trial lawyer in the universe, or earning a million dollars this year. A creative idea might be as simple as discovering an excellent starting paragraph in something you are writing or discovering how to rearrange the shoes in your closet. It's anything to which you say, "Hey, that's a good idea."

2) PRIME THE PUMP

Why do you get good ideas rather than not? That is , when an idea pops into your head, why did that particular idea come to you? The answer is that you have "primed the pump." That is, you have given your brain a few problems or things to work on subconsciously, and that's why solutions come during quiet times.

The way you give your brain things to work on is an approach to problem-solving which some of us use instinctively, but which I want to make explicit here: identify specific questions, problems or needs you have. Identify all of the things you *don't* know about a problem, all the questions that would need to be answered for the problem to be resolved. These questions are the stuff that the subconscious works on and about which we get answers, solutions, and insights during creative periods. So priming the pump means to identify what you don't know or aren't clear about, verbalize it (generally on paper), and allow it to be in your subconscious.

What goes through our mind when we daydream? They are generally those things that we have been actively thinking about, working on, or having concerns about. Our brain manipulates what we have been concerned about, takes new input and uses it to resolve problems. We get good ideas because we have a need for those ideas. We create needs by verbalizing them, by actually putting into words our problems, our questions, things that annoy us, things that are missing, things that we want. Creating a space to know by identifying in words what you *don't* know is what starts the creative process.

Here are two practical exercises you can do for valence-setting or priming the pump. First, make an anxiety list. I spoke about this process earlier. Clear your mind by putting everything that's on your mind down on paper. You might start any creative session by doing that, by just clearing your mind. Then, after you have everything that you're anxious about at work or in your personal life on paper, sit there with the list and don't *try* to resolve anything.

There is a difference between "trying to resolve" a problem and "being in the presence of" a problem. During the creative period, we need to be in the presence of problems. In other words, just look at and notice them; don't force yourself to try to resolve any particular problem. Let your mind go where it naturally wants to, whether it's on your biggest problem or not. This allows your right brain to work much more freely and creatively to produce clarifications and answers to problems. Often in this process you may be hoping for an answer to anxiety number one, and what your brain gives you is an answer to anxiety number six. Be grateful for what it gives you.

The second method of valence-setting is for working on a specific problem or anxiety on your list: Pick your top problem and identify everything you know about it and everything you don't know about it. The simplest way to do that is to either write or dictate everything that you have to say about the problem or issue in a free-flow of ideas. Every time you come to something that you don't know, something that confuses or puzzles you, something you don't understand, a blockage, a question that you need answered, identify it as a question. At the end of dictating, you might have six or twenty-six questions concerning an individual problem.

Don't *try* to answer those questions. Simply sit in the presence of the questions and let your mind go where it wants to. It might not want to play with that problem. Allow it to flow wherever it wants to and see what it comes up with. The idea is to be creative, not to try to resolve problems. Creativity takes its own course. As long as your mind produces ideas for you, accept the ideas it gives to you.

COMPLETION: GET IT DONE

The second C is Completion. I spoke about this extensively in Chapter Three of Section Four. A simple technique to start completing things is: Make a list of everything that's incomplete for you. In fact, make two lists—a work list and a personal list. This is very similar to the anxiety list I just spoke of. If an item pops up in your mind and on to your list, that means it's incomplete, something that you've been thinking about and haven't finished. Once you finish making your list, set a time frame to complete every item on the list. I am currently working on a list of thirty-one incompletions. I'm about half way through and have six days to go.

There are three ways to attack your incompletion list:

1) Set a certain amount of time aside each day to work on the list, say one hour per day for personal items and three hours a day for work items.

2) Commit to completing a certain number of items per day. For instance, complete one item on your personal list and two items on your work list each day. This creates control or orderliness about attacking a list. Also, in tackling the incompletions for the day, choose a reward for accomplishing them. For example, if you complete two items, take a fifteen minute walk, or call a friend you haven't called in a long time, or play with a project that really would be fun for you. The things we choose as rewards are usually those things that allow us to be creative, to play and to have fun.

3) Make a commitment to do something about each item on the list. Move it forward in some way, even if it's just talking to somebody about the issue. Give yourself a deadline for having done something about each issue.

As you're working through the list, other incompletions will pop up. *Don't* put them on the same list. Start making another list. Otherwise, you'll never have the satisfaction of completing your original "incompletion list." If there are thirty-one items originally, then leave it at thirty-one. So there will be a finite date in time when you can say: "I have completed all thirty-one items; I have completed my incompletion list."

CONTROL: HOW TO GET CONTROL

How do we create the third C, control, in our lives? I have answered this question in Section Four, in the same chapters that deal with completion. Obviously control is intimately related to completion. I discussed the ways to control your day, control your anxieties, control paperwork, control piles, and so on. However, control can become an end it itself. We love to impose order on things. Organizing is a pleasureful activity in itself. How do you know when you have too little control or too much control?

You have too little control if you are in a constant state of anxiety, things are always on your mind, there is always disorder on your desk or in your house or in your work-space. You don't have a peaceful sense about moving through your work and being in control of it. You have more of a sense that your work is controlling you.

On the other hand, you know that you have too much control when you start getting bored. I have a friend who says her mother-in-law knows how many slices of bread are left in the loaf! You get bored when you are not producing anything new, anything exciting. That is because creativity is missing. You also have too much control if you aren't completing things, if you seem to be forever getting organized but never completing anything. In the final analysis, if you never have order, something's wrong, and if you always have order something's wrong.

CONCLUSION

Control and completion are the base which allows us to create. If there are too many incompletions or too little control, we don't have a solid base to stand on from which we can create. The temptation for 90% of us is to always be building the base and never spending any time to create. For the other 10%, it's always creating and never building a base by controlling or completing.

In summary, how can you feel that you have a balance between creation, control and completion in your life? The answer is to be aware of the need for these three things in your life, and to monitor your satisfaction level. If you are feeling dissatisfaction, it's usually because one of these is lacking.

Perhaps at the beginning of each day you can declare it to be primarily a creation day, a control day, or a completion day. Or you might say: I want a piece of each of these in my day; how can I achieve that? It's also helpful to have an outside coach to talk to once a week. This would give you the opportunity to look back at the previous week to monitor your satisfaction level and to see if you gave adequate time for each of the three C's. Then you can create a plan to achieve them in the coming week. The ultimate measure of balance is your own sense of satisfaction.

AFFIRMATIONS

Balancing the Three C's

❖ I create. I control. I complete.

❖ Whatever I choose to do now serves a value.

❖ Creation (control, completion) is how I achieve my purpose in life.

❖ I am innately creative.

❖ I have the habit of completion.

CHAPTER 44

HOW TO CREATE SATISFACTION #7:
A PRACTICAL PROBLEM-SOLVING APPLICATION —
THE CRITICAL ELEMENT METHOD

The method I use at some of my workshops to help people create satisfaction in their lives is called "The Critical Element Method." You can use it right now.

First, make a list on paper of all of the things that prevent you from being satisfied. You may want to make two lists, one for work and one for your personal life. Then, select the most important item on each list. Generally, most of your dissatisfaction comes from a few key or critical items, often one critical item. Even if there is more than one critical item, you can only deal with one item at a time, so you might as well define which is the most important, the critical element, and work on that. If you can't choose between five that are equally critical, close your eyes, put your finger on your list and pick the one it falls nearest to.

Once you select the item that dissatisfies you the most, ask the question: "What is it that prevents me from reaching this goal or resolving this problem?" Write down all the answers that occur to you. This is your second list. Then identify which is the most important element on *this* list.

Now you have a new critical element, and you ask the same question you asked above for this new critical element: What prevents me from reaching *this* goal or resolving *this* problem?

How to Create Satisfaction

Write the answers. This is now your third list.

Then identify the most important element on this list and again ask about that element: What prevents me from reaching *this* goal or resolving *this* problem? Continue to repeat this process until you have nothing to write any more.

As you can see, the critical element method is a method for breaking down complex situations into simple ones. The method simply repeats the three-step process: Make a list, select the critical element and ask what prevents you from reaching this goal or resolving this problem. The process helps you to identify barriers to moving forward and to target the one which is most critical.

To illustrate how the process works and to get some insights into the thinking process, here are some examples of how workshop participants applied the critical element process. In each example, item number one on the list is what prevented the person from being satisfied or productive. Item number two is the critical element that prevented number one from happening. Item number three is the critical element that prevented number two from happening and so on.

Example A:

Critical Element:
1) Too much work to do; can't finish work on time.
Why Not Resolved:
2) Accepting new clients.
Why Not Resolved:
3) Terminating largest client.

Example B:

1) More family time needed.
2) Heavy work load.
3) My insufficient delegation.
4) Heavy work load on my supervisory group which strains their available time.
5) Need to redesign systems, automate more processes, eliminate some tasks.

Example C:

1) Strengthening marital relationship.
2) Open communication.
3) Dislike of spouse's questioning attitude.
4) View of myself as a competent decision-maker.
5) Lack of commitment to share authority and responsibility in a relationship.

In each of these three examples, the person worked down to the point of taking a specific action. Since they went no further down their list, I presume there is no barrier to carrying out the actions they came up with. If I were speaking with each of these individuals I would ask, "Are you going to do it, or is there something that prevents you from doing it?" For example: (A) Are you going to terminate your largest client? (B) Are you going to redesign your systems? (C) Are you going to make a commitment to share? If the answer was "No", I would ask: What prevents you from doing it? That is, I would continue the critical element process. If they said they were going to do it, I would ask them when. So, if you actually try this process, you should reach a point where you are willing to take action.

The other option besides taking action would be to choose the current situation. This goes back to the "change it or choose it" policy. For example, in Example A, perhaps the person might choose to not terminate his largest client. Then it would be clear that the person needed to stop taking in new clients or be satisfied with not finishing work on time. When put so boldly (not to finish work on time), choosing the current situation probably would not be acceptable. So, the need to take action becomes obvious.

Through these examples, we can see that creating greater satisfaction or productivity often starts with action. If these three people carry out these actions, will it resolve their problem? Will they become satisfied and productive? The answer is: We don't know. What I am sure of, though, is that if they carry out these actions they will be on the road to greater satisfaction and productivity. Why? Because they will be in action. When you are in action, you find out whether the action you are taking is the appropriate one. If it's not, you come up with the next action.

So, there are two possible results in using the critical element method to resolve problems. The most important is that it often gets people to break through the complexity of problems into some specific measurable action. The second result may be that they change their attitude about the problem.

Let's take a look at two more sequences of the critical element method where attitude change is the resolution.

Example D:

1) Better ability to handle paper and keep work space orga-nized.
2) Too busy to take the time to organize.
3) Not having someone to delegate work to or not knowing how to delegate the work.
4) "I can do it quicker and better" philosophy.

Example E:

1) Disciplining myself to focus on what is most important and then do it without procrastination.
2) Overcome fear of rejection for putting time into client development.
3) Overcome guilt feelings for focusing on *my* priorities and not the priorities of others.

From these two examples, we can see that what may be re-quired is not taking action, but a change of attitude. In the first case, what's required is to give up the attitude, "I can do it quicker and better." Better yet, it would not be to give up this attitude, but to incorporate it into a larger attitude: "Yes, I can do it quicker and better now, but if I continue to do this I will never have time to do those things that are more important to me. Therefore, it's better that I trade off my need for perfection and invest some time in delegating initially, so that in the long run I can be working on what's more important and produce more results."

In the second example above, the shift of attitude would be: "I will not feel guilty about focusing on my priorities." Better yet, it would be: "I acknowledge that I feel guilty when working on my priorities and not others', but I will live with this guilt because I know that what I am doing will produce more results for me and for my company in the long run."

In both of these cases producing satisfaction comes about not by taking action but by shifting attitude. Once the attitude shifts, then the action follows. In the first case, the person will start to delegate. In the second case the person will spend time on client development.

It is equally possible that the attitude shift would work in the opposite direction. For example, in the first case the person might decide, "Yes, I can do things quicker and better and so I will continue to do them that way. Therefore, I will make the trade-off with handling paper better and keeping my work space organized, because I choose to do my own work rather than delegate it." In the second case the person might say, "Yes, I feel guilty for not doing what others want me to do, so I will simply do what others want me to do since they run the company." So in both cases the attitude shift is in giving up the expectation and choosing to accept the status quo—although it seems unlikely in both cases.

Which is the appropriate choice in these two cases—attitude shift or action? The answer is: Whichever you pick. Whatever the person chooses is what's appropriate. Whatever they say will make them more satisfied or more productive is appropriate. What if they make a mistake? It will become clear to them and they will make the next choice. There are no set rules which one should follow, except to pursue one's own satisfaction. What the critical element method does is to have you come to a point where you can see the trade-off that you must make. It leads to a simple bottom line: In the end, all you have are your options and your decision. Your options are to take action or change attitudes: Have what you choose or choose what you have. Satisfaction comes from making the choice.

HOW TO ELIMINATE CIRCULAR AND FALSE REASONING (AND STOP BEATING YOURSELF UP)

There is a third possible outcome to using the critical element method. That is, you may come to a dead end where there doesn't seem to be a clear choice about either changing attitude or taking action. This is often the result of one of two types of dead-end reasoning: Circular reasoning or false reasoning.

To illustrate, let's first take a look at circular reasoning in this example of a critical element process:

Example F:

1) Better budgeting of time.
2) No time to do it - the tyranny of the urgent.
3) Everyone's business is important to him; it all must be done.
4) I run out of time, and end up putting out brush fires.
5) I run out of energy.
6) I need rest and relaxation.
7) Lack of time.

This is circular reasoning. The person keeps coming back to lack of time. (Numbers two, four and seven.) If you find yourself caught up in circular reasoning, then you need to define the element that keeps coming up. For example, in this case, what does "lack of time" really mean? As I discussed earlier, it probably means one of the following: I don't set priorities; I don't say no to people; I let myself be interrupted whenever someone has a need. Redefinition means looking at the choices I am making that keep me in this situation. Unless we look at specific choices rather than generalizations about them, we will always be entrapped, running in a circle. Once we define the generalization (lack of time) into one or more of the three specifics mentioned above, we can return to the critical element method: Which of these three is most important, and what prevents me from resolving it?

The second type of dead-end reasoning is false reasoning. It is illustrated in the following:

Example G:

1) Better organization.
2) Prioritizing.
3) Interruptions/distractions.
4) Self-discipline.

Phrases that identify "character flaws" such as "lack of self-discipline" are an example of false reasoning. They include such phrases as "undisciplined, lacking confidence, not motivated, lazy," etc. These are labels that don't move thinking forward, but are actually an excuse for not taking responsibility. I discussed eliminating this "name-calling" in the chapter on procrastination. All that saying "I lack discipline" adds to the conversation is guilt: "I don't control interruptions and I am a bad person as a result." It is more accurate to say: "I don't control interruptions because I choose not to. I am free to take action to control them in the future, or not to, and thus accept being less organized."

False reasoning is actually another form of circular reasoning. Look at this example:

- I don't do something.
- Why? I am lazy.
- What is the evidence that I'm lazy?
- I don't do things that I (or others) feel I should do.
- Why don't I do those things? Because I'm lazy.

Name-calling doesn't lead anywhere. A clearer way of thinking is this: "I didn't do X because I chose not to do it. I chose to do Y." This takes responsibility for the action and eliminates the "name-calling" and the self-criticism which is its essence.

Eliminating name-calling from your vocabulary will be more responsible, will make you feel better and will also prevent the critical element method from going off track. For example, when asked, "What prevents you from doing this?" you answer, "I'm lazy." The next question is a non-question: "What makes you lazy?" or "What prevents you from not being lazy?" These are not useful questions because they get you into psychological guessing games which will not bear fruit either in action or peace of mind. What we need to do is to circumvent the whole discussion by catching the use of the word "lazy" or any other name-calling and eliminating it.

In summary, what the critical element method helps us to do is take responsibility for our own satisfaction. It helps us to isolate what prevents us from being satisfied and to either take action or change our attitude. It helps us to redefine things when we are trapped in circular or self-defeating reasoning. In short, it helps us to create satisfaction by looking at what's so and to change it or choose it.

AFFIRMATION

Resolving Problems

❖ There are no big problems, only groups of little decisions.

❖ I get to the essence of every problem.

❖ Creating satisfaction for myself is totally in my control.

CHAPTER 45

HOW TO MEASURE
AND PRODUCE SATISFACTION DAILY

In my workshops, I often ask people to rate themselves on a scale of 1 to 10 concerning their level of satisfaction in work. It is very difficult for people to give themselves a 10. How can you rate yourself a "10 out of 10" in satisfaction? Measuring satisfaction may be confusing. Let's look at four cases concerning measuring satisfaction:

1) You may have just accomplished a long term goal you have been striving for. For example, you get a new position, you get a degree or you successfully finish a long project. In each of these cases, if you were to give yourself a rating out of 10, you would probably give yourself a 10. However, if I were to ask you six months later about your satisfaction level, it might be lower. The further away from achieving an accomplishment, the less it means. In this sense satisfaction is always fleeting. You may give yourself a 10 for an instant, but then it disappears.

2) You are working on some big goals or problems, and you give yourself a 7 or 8 on a scale of 10 because the goals haven't been reached or the problems haven't been re-

solved. Yet, you are moving toward the goals or toward resolving the problems. In other words, you are "on the way." You are satisfied with the progress you're making in moving toward your destination. Yet, you don't give yourself a 10 because you're not there yet.

3) You give yourself a rating of 5 or less. Generally, this kind of rating means not only that you aren't satisfied with end results, but you aren't even satisfied with the progress you are making. In other words, you are really dissatisfied.

4) You give yourself a 7 or 8 because you have many aspects to your work (and life); some are good, some not so good. For example, you might give yourself a 10 for the technical part of your work, but a 4 for relations with your boss. So you come up with an average rating of 7. In order to give yourself a 10, you need everything to be satisfactory at the same time. This seems almost impossible.

Perhaps we need to look at the overall picture of our work and / or of our life and give ourselves a 10 because of this attitude: "There are many things I want to achieve, and I can't achieve all of them at the same time. Therefore, I am focusing on the ones that make the most difference to me (the critical elements), and I am moving forward satisfactorily in those areas. I am moving forward not only in quantitative goals but also in qualitative goals—being in control of my work rather than controlled by it, having time for family, relaxation, for creative thinking. I am moving forward satisfactorily in the areas that make the most difference to me, so I give myself a 10 in satisfaction."

In short, to be able to give yourself a 10, all you have to be able to say is, "I am moving satisfactorily in the right direction. Many people have unrealistic expectations. They would prefer not to live in this world. They say, "I would like to be independently wealthy, to play golf every day, to play well enough to be in the pros, to be the leading player on the pro tour. Since I can't have these, or have them all, or have them all at once, I am dissatisfied." Good luck! In the real world you can have *any*thing you want, but you can't have *every*thing you want. You have to make choices. As long as you are making choices, and moving toward what's important, give yourself a 10!

I find that most people are too demanding on themselves. They can never be satisfied; they would never give themselves a 10. The question to confront is: What do you expect of yourself? What would it take for you to be a 10? If you don't know the answer, you are condemned to a life of dissatisfaction, a life of scarcity: "Whatever I have, do and am is not enough." It is going through life with a "never enough" attitude: I achieved a lot; it was never enough. The alternative is: I am always satisfied, and I always want more. I am always a 10.

HOW TO BE SATISFIED EACH DAY

How does one get out of this kind of self-defeating thinking? A very simple, yet, key question you can ask yourself at the end of each day is: "Would I have done anything differently today?" If, in reviewing our day, we discover there is something we would have done differently, then we have learned a lesson for the coming day. If we find that we wouldn't have done anything differently, then we need to give ourselves a 10 in satisfaction for that day.

Many of us are possessed by free-floating anxiety, guilt or self-criticism. (Perhaps that's what "possession by the Devil" in past centuries really meant.) It's the nagging thought: I could have done it better; I could have done it differently. The way to ground yourself in reality is to simply ask: "In what way? In what way could I have done it better or differently?" If you come up with an answer to the question, then you've learned. If you don't come up with an answer, then you know that your free-floating anxiety is speaking. The way to control this anxiety is to make a positive affirmation: "I have spent this day in the best way possible; there is nothing I would have changed to make it better."

Even better than questioning yourself about satisfaction at the end of the day is questioning yourself at the beginning of the day. That is, look ahead at your day and decide what it will take to create satisfaction for yourself. I have five simple questions you can ask yourself at the beginning of each day, preferably on tape, to assure that you go home satisfied. I call the process Sanitate's Satisfaction

Tape or the Morning Clearing Tape. Here is the exercise.

SANITATE'S SATISFACTION TAPE

Answer the following questions at the beginning of each morning on tape. You can also write them out, but a tape is much faster. You don't listen to the tape afterwards; you just tape over it again the next day. It is the act of speaking that makes the difference. The questions are a way of clearing your head and focusing on creating satisfaction. Here are the five questions:

1) How do I feel physically: A, B, or C?
2) Why did I give myself that rating?
3) How do I feel psychologically: A, B, or C?
4) What's on my mind?
5) What do I need to do to feel satisfied today?

I have been using these questions for many years. I used to use them every work day, and I suggest you do that if you are going to try the exercise. At this point in my life I find myself much clearer and more energetic each day, so I only do this exercise when I need to. Now I only use it when I am sluggish, when I don't feel like working, when I don't have a lot of energy to move forward, when I need to clear my head.

Let's look at the questions more closely:

1) How do I feel physically: A, B, or C? Feel free to use a plus or minus. The purpose of this question is to get you in touch with your body. We often walk around thinking that our body is one thing and our mind is another thing. And yet, we are one. I often find that many of my problems which I thought were psychological are really physical. The following four causes are probably the source of 95% of your (and the world's) problems: I am hungry; I am tired; I am constipated; or I have P.M.S. (Men can have P.M.S. too—a chemical or biological imbalance in the body.) Think about it! Stress is a combination of psychological and physical factors. We need to start noticing and taking better care of our physical well-being.

2) Why did I give myself that rating? This helps you to be more specific about what is actually happening with your body or whether anything is ailing you. Is it your head, your back, your stomach, your overall energy level? I have actually gone home from work twice after answering this question, once with the flu and once to get badly needed sleep. After sleeping two or three hours I went back to the office and accomplished more that afternoon than I would have accomplished the whole day if I had stayed at work.

3) How do I rate myself psychologically: A, B, or C? This is an early morning satisfaction evaluation. I find that I never give myself an "A" on this question. The reason is that if I'm an "A" I don't do this exercise. I just move forward into what I want to do that day. But I use the tape when something is bothering me, physically or psychologically —when I'm feeling down, frustrated, annoyed, etc. This rating gives you your overall feeling, and the next question gets down to specifics.

4) What's on my mind? This is another way of saying: Why did I just give myself that rating for number three? Generally, when I ask this question, I have my To Do List in front of me. Many of the things on my mind are simply things to do, so I get them out of my head onto paper. Other things on my mind, though, are problems, conflicts, unresolved issues, etc. Saying them on tape helps me to identify consciously what may be going on subconsciously. I don't do anything about the issues or problems at that point. I simply identify them on tape.

5) What do I need to do to feel satisfied today? This is the key question in the process. It is a natural development from answering the first four questions. They ground me in the reality of knowing how I feel physically and psychologically and why. My satisfaction must take place within this reality. Another way of asking the question is: Given what is going on for me physically and psychologically right

now, what do I need to do to feel satisfied? Asking this question makes me totally responsible for my own satisfaction. If I wait and hope for the universe to come in and satisfy me, I'm pretty sure I will be doomed to failure. However, if I acknowledge that I am responsible for my own satisfaction, then I will create the way to achieve that satisfaction. If you want to go home satisfied, you have to start by asking what it will take for you to go home satisfied.

The process doesn't take long—5 minutes or less. Try it for at least a week and see what you learn about yourself, and see whether it propels you into creating greater satisfaction each day. The purpose of using a tape is simply to get the words out. There is a vast difference between thinking about something and verbalizing about it. Verbalization forces subconsciousness into consciousness. Consciousness at the beginning of the day will make it much more likely that you will give yourself a 10 at the end of the day.

Be careful what you do with the tape, by the way. One day my secretary came in with my tape and said: "I don't think I'm supposed to be typing this." She was right!

CHAPTER 46

HOW TO MEASURE AND PRODUCE SATISFACTION EACH MOMENT, EACH MONTH, AND EACH LIFE

I have been discussing measuring satisfaction on a daily basis. Next let's look at satisfaction in both the shortest and longest time frames—in the moment and in life—and from a monthly time frame as well.

HOW TO BE SATISFIED EACH MOMENT

If, at the end of the day, you are not sure whether you would have done anything differently, you are not conscious of how you are spending the parts of the day. In order to be clear about the whole day, we need to be clear about the parts. That means we need to be satisfied with each activity. If you are not moving happily and smoothly through each activity, some thought is lurking in your mind that needs to be confronted.

As I discussed earlier, the demon thought might possess us, "Whatever I am doing, it's wrong." Or, "Whatever I am doing, I should be doing something else. If I am doing A, I should be doing B, and if I'm doing B, I should be doing A." The way to exorcise this demon is to simply make the decision: What I am doing is clearly the best thing to be doing because I say so—unless it's clearly *not* the best thing to be doing! If you're not sure what is the best, declare what you're doing *now* to be the best.

How to Create Satisfaction

The second way of examining yourself in the moment is to deal with the demon that says, "However I am doing it, it's wrong. There must be a better way." In this case it's not *what* I'm doing that's wrong, but *how* I'm doing it. We need the same kind of questioning to exorcise this demon: Do you know a better way to be doing it? If so, do it. If not, make the affirmation that the way you are doing it is the best possible way. If there really *is* a better way, the process of doing it the way you're doing it now will show you the better way.

We often lead our lives thinking that there is a book about life somewhere called "The Best Way," and it gives the best way to do everything. We think our problem is that we just haven't read the book, or we've read it and forgotten what it said! The reality, though, is that there is no such book. The book you should read is "Life Is an Experiment." What this book says is: There are no rules for human behavior. There is just experimenting in doing things— and finding better and better ways of doing them. It is the action of doing that brings forth the better way, not the better way that brings forth the action.

Let me back off a bit. There are, in fact, books of rules for human behavior. But these rules are simply statements of what we now see as the better way. They come *after* the doing. They *are* the better way, until something better comes along! To create satisfaction in the moment, we need to reverse the statement from "Whatever I'm doing is wrong," to "Whatever I'm doing is right." If you discover a better way in the doing, do it the better way.

What I am *not* suggesting in this section is that we engage in an on-going moment-by-moment self-evaluation: "Am I satisfied? Am I satisfied?" This kind of constant questioning can be a great source of *dis*satisfaction. Rather, periodically during the day, we take a pulse of our well-being. If we notice dissatisfaction, we deal with it. If we don't, we simply look at what's next. Probably the most satisfied people in life are those who never even consider their satisfaction. They are so happily caught up each moment in living that they don't think about satisfaction—they are just satisified!

The next question is: "If I am creating satisfaction moment by moment, how do I know that I am not sacrificing long term satisfaction for short term satisfaction?"

HOW TO BE SATISFIED EACH MONTH

To handle this question, I suggest that once a month you pull back and look to see whether you're achieving your long-term goals. I suggest once a month because it's a regular period of time. The best way to do this is to use a monthly To Do List. First, create a list of things that you want to do. Group them into categories. For example, many of the tasks that I want to do each month fall under one of the following categories: marketing workshops, teaching workshops, developing workshops, writing, volunteer work and administrative work. Then use one of two methods to deal with the list.

The first is the traditional time management method: Set priorities and follow them. The second is: Look at your priorities in each category and then do what you're drawn to do each day. At the end of the month come back to review what you've completed and what you haven't. Then give yourself a satisfaction rating for each category and for the whole month. For example, concerning marketing, I may have completed eight out of ten tasks, but still give myself a fifty percent rating since I didn't attack the most important task. Or, conversely, I might have done only two tasks but I might give myself a ninety percent rating because I followed a new marketing opportunity which wasn't even on my list. Perhaps you completed ten out of ten goals in an area but hated doing it. You might give yourself a 100% rating on satisfaction because, although you didn't enjoy the process, you're exhilarated because you accomplished the tasks. On the other hand, you might give yourself only a 50% rating because the accomplishment was almost not worth the effort.

So rating your satisfaction in each area really enables you to look at the bigger picture. I don't necessarily advocate giving actual numerical ratings for each area, although that may be useful for some people. What I do advocate is to take each area of your work and ask: Am I satisfied with what happened here this month? And, am I satisfied with the month as a whole, with the balance between all of these areas?

You might also apply this evaluation to the non-work part of your life: What satisfaction rating would I give my life for the past month? Maybe your work didn't go so well, but your relations with your family went wonderfully, your church committee produced a great event and you had a new low in your golf score. Too much self-evaluation can become tedious, but periodically it can help us to look at and balance all the pieces of our life.

I used this quote from a Jesuit earlier, "Experience without reflection is not educative; it's just one damn thing after another." Our lives often get caught up in doing one thing after another. We need to step back periodically and say: How do I evaluate my life? How satisfactory has it been in the last month? This gives us an opportunity to see if our whole life is moving forward.

HOW TO BE SATISFIED EACH LIFE

We have looked at daily satisfaction, moment by moment satisfaction and monthly satisfaction. Now let's look at satisfaction over a lifetime. I used "each life" in the title of this section to be consistent with previous section headings. However, maybe we *do* come back again! Whether we do or not, the key to being satisfied in life is to accept the *relativity* of life—which I discussed in the chapter on "The Scarcity of Life."

Just as at the end of the day, at the end of life we can ask: Would I have spent this life differently? Put in this light, the question seems ludicrous. The answer doesn't make any difference! Actually, on one's death bed, it might make a difference as to whether one dies peacefully or not. The way to die peacefully is to affirm your life. It is to say, I have lived the best possible life I could have. Yet this may bring up the thought: But there *are* things I would have done differently, it's just that it's too late now. In this case, the thing to do is to forgive yourself for what you would have changed, and to affirm your life as it is—acknowledge what *is*, what you have made of your life, not what *isn't*.

The privilege of being human is that we can anticipate this question of satisfaction in life (would I have lived my life differently?) *before* reaching our deathbed, and we can forestall having to answer it negatively. Let's take a closer look at how we can prevent ourselves from looking back at life with regret. Here is a scenario of a dialogue on how to eliminate regret—"I would have, could have, should have":

"If I could choose again, I would choose differently."

"Why didn't you choose differently back then?"

"I was too insecure (too dumb, too stubborn, too drunk, too angry, etc.) to do so."

"Did you know that you were too insecure?"

"No."

"Then, given that you were insecure, did you do the best you could have?"

"Yes, but if I had just been thinking clearly, I would surely not have done what I did."

"Were you thinking clearly at that point?"

"No."

"Then, given the way you were—not thinking clearly—you did the best you could?"

"Yes."

Self-forgiveness is in a lot shorter supply than forgiveness of others. The only way to deal with the past is to forgive ourselves and affirm ourselves: I did the best I could; I did the *best!* Asking forgiveness of others may be in order to complete the past, but it goes hand in hand with forgiving and affirming ourselves.

This discussion brings me to a deeper level of looking at what we are really talking about when we talk about "the past." People say: "The past is dead." This is true but let's take it one step further: There is no such thing as the past. Life is a succession of "now's." All that exists of the past now is our memories. So, the past has no reality except in our heads.

If the memories are plaguing us, the only way to deal with them is to put them to rest. How does one do that? By affirming the present or taking action for the future. In other words, if you are regretting something that is gone and unchangeable, affirm yourself now. If it is an on-going situation that you can still change, that you can do something about, then do it. For example, you might say, "I did not give myself enough time to work on my important projects today; therefore, I will give myself more time tomorrow." Or, "I didn't give enough time to developing new clients last month; therefore, I will spend more time on client development this month." Or, "I haven't communicated with my children the way I wanted to; therefore, I will do it now." The only value of negative thoughts about the past is to change the present. Since the past doesn't exist, at any given moment you can absolutely affirm yourself in the present: "I am the best person I can be; I'm doing what's best now."

From a religious viewpoint, one might say: Don't we need to ask God's forgiveness for past wrong-doings or stupidities? The answer is yes, as long as it helps us to forgive ourselves and affirm ourselves in the present. God, after all, if he (or she) really is God, doesn't care. His satisfaction at seeing the grand design of the universe fulfill itself is not dependent on what we did do or didn't do. Even grand-scale Hitlerian atrocities are a blip in the unfolding of the universe. What Hitler needed to do, by the way, was forgive himself and ask forgiveness from others. Had he done this early in life, perhaps those atrocities would never have come to pass. The only *you* that exists is the *you* that exists now, in the present. The only proper attitude towards the *you* existing now is forgiveness and affirmation.

Memories are electrochemical charges stored in your brain. But we give them power. They live on not only in our consciousness, but perhaps more importantly in our subconsciousness. Much of our action in the present is living out scripts and decisions that we made in the past.

Since many books have been written about this, I make two suggestions. The first I've discussed earlier: if you seem to be trapped in self-destructive behavior—addictions, inability to form relationships, etc.—the thing to do is get professional help. Secondly, if current dissatisfaction seems to come from a past event that you remember, clean up the past event. That means going back to the person involved in the past event and communicating with him or her. If this is not possible, then make a conscious act of declaring the event complete. Generally, it is our unexpressed feelings that get us stuck in memories of past events. Once those feelings and what we think and what we want have been expressed, the memory of the past event no longer controls the present.

By bringing this discussion on satisfaction to the ultimate, to the end of life, we come around full circle: You may be a 10 today, but tomorrow you are not. The nature of satisfaction is that it's not so much *what* you achieve, but the process of achieving. The ultimate question and test of satisfaction is: Am I enjoying the process? I love the quote, "He who has the most toys when he dies wins." In the book, *The Best Way*, there is a list of every human being, and it gives exactly how many toys each should have in life and what those toys should be. The catch is that nobody gets to read this book until after they die! By the way, I got to read a draft copy of the book, and it says that so far you are doing things just right.

The bottom line for giving yourself a 10 in satisfaction in life comes down to making affirmations—to affirm that what you're doing is always the best unless you're clear it's not the best. This applies to instant-by-instant decisions, daily satisfaction and satisfaction in life. More importantly it comes down to affirming not only that what I am doing is the best, but also that I *am* the best at any given moment; I *am* a 10.

AFFIRMATIONS

Measuring Satisfaction

❖ Whatever I'm doing now is the best; how I'm doing it is best.

❖ When I see how I can do better, I do better; when I don't, what I am doing is the best.

❖ I am completely satisfied with what I create each day.

❖ Each month I move forward the main areas of my work and life in balance.

❖ My life is perfect.

❖ I am perfect.

CHAPTER 47

HOW TO MEASURE YOUR PRODUCTIVITY

Let's spend a moment to discuss how to measure productivity. How can I be a "10" in productivity?

Initially, I suggest you work through my audio tapes and workbook on time management. They give you dozens of specific actions you can take to become more productive. You can use the form in the back of the book to order them. Here, I will explore the attitude shift necessary to be a "10" in productivity.

To rate yourself as a 10 in productivity, you need to ask the question: How do I know I'm being as productive as I could be? In work there are several bottom-line answers: Are we making a profit? Are we growing? Is my division or department reaching its quotas and goals? Am I reaching my quotas and goals? These are the questions that ground you in the reality of whether you're being productive or not.

What I am more concerned about here, however, is the *feeling* of productivity. Often in my workshops I find people who say they could never be a 10 in productivity. If they produce a million dollars, it's not enough. If they double that, it's not enough, and so on. I spent a good deal of time talking about scarcity in the first part of this book. The feeling of scarcity or inadequacy prevents us from giving ourselves a 10. How do you overcome that? The way to be a 10 in productivity is the same as achieving a 10 in satisfaction—affirm you are a 10. All of us could work longer, but can you work smarter? If yes, then do it. If not, affirm that you are being as productive as you can be now.

To make the transition from affirming scarcity to affirming abundance, I suggest a set of questions and a set of measures to use to become satisfied with your productivity. The first set are general questions to help ground you. They are:

1) Am I in action? Am I *doing* something?

2) Is what I'm doing producing results? Am I actually accomplishing something, or am I spinning my wheels?

3) Are the results I'm producing the ones I really want to produce? Do they tie into my long range or overall goals? Are they making a difference in my life?

4) Are the results I am producing lessening the *quality* of my life? In other words, even though I am achieving my quantitative goals, are my qualitative goals suffering? Is the process of achievement enjoyable? Or is my productivity actually creating stress in my life and taking away from my satisfaction rather than contributing to it?

These are questions to ask yourself periodically. In taking a backward look, the bottom line is to ask: Would I have done anything differently? If the answer is no, give yourself a 10 for productivity.

But that's *after* the fact. How do you decide on how to be productive *before* you tackle a project? How do you gear yourself up so you can move forward at an intensity that's satisfying, so you can have the appropriate balance between underwork and overwork? The answer is to decide to which of three levels of productivity you want to commit.

THE THREE LEVELS OF COMMITMENT FOR PRODUCTIVITY

The three levels of commitment for productivity are three ways of measuring how much you want to produce. They are successively easier ways of getting you to move forward and measure what you produce. The three types of commitment you can make are: a results commitment, an action commitment, or a time commitment. Going from the hardest to the easiest, they are:

1) Results: a commitment to achieving the total results or goal by a given time.

2) Action: a commitment to carrying out some action to move toward the goal by a given time.

3) Time: a commitment to put in a certain amount of time in carrying out activities directed to achieving the goal.

Which of these levels you choose depends on what you see as necessary to create satisfaction for yourself at any given time. Of course, you also have the option to choose to do nothing. Whichever of these three you pick, you can then rate yourself a 10 in productivity if you achieve that level.

I'll give you an example of how these three work from a viewpoint of selling. I might make a Results commitment: To sell five days of my workshops this week; or an Action commitment: To make twenty sales calls on the phone a day; or a Time commitment: To spend two hours a day in making sales calls. Each of these levels is successively easier, but they all move you forward.

The first level is a commitment to results no matter what. So I might spend four hours on the first day, and if I'm not selling any workshops I might go up to six or eight hours the next day, or ten or twelve hours. If I were putting in this time and effort and still achieving no results, I would pull back and re-evaluate what I was doing and force myself to get some advice, or change my game plan, or both. The benefit to a results commitment is that you produce the results you want to produce. The drawback is that you may pay a price in terms of all your other desires and commitments in order to achieve those results.

On the second level you're not committed to producing the results but to taking actions or steps you think will produce the results. If from past history your average is one sale per twenty calls, you know that if you make twenty calls a day for five days you ought to be able to sell five workshops. However, there is no guarantee that you will sell five days, you may sell zero or you may sell ten. But your commitment is to take the action of making the calls. The twenty calls may take you two or three or four hours, but you're committed to making them.

The third level is the easiest level. You're committed to putting in the time. Your intention is that the time you put in will be in effective action, and that the action will produce results. But, what you're committing to is to make those calls for two hours a day, whether that turns out to be five calls or twenty-five calls, and whether it results in no sales or ten sales.

The trick is to determine which of these three levels of commitment to action will turn you on, will create satisfaction for you in any given day or on any given task. I find that I vary between these three levels. I spend most of my time on the second level, some of my time on the third level and a little of my time on the first level. In the past, I used to put great pressure on myself when I was committed to producing results. However, even though I may have produced the results, I didn't get satisfaction. Conversely, sometimes I get exhilaration from producing results, no matter what the cost or output.

I remember one time several years ago when I had the goal of clearing up all of my work before going on vacation. I completed my work, got to bed at 4:00 a.m. and got up two hours later to leave for vacation. I felt exhilarated about the achievement, and didn't feel that the cost was high. Most of the time now, though, I am satisfied by making an action or time commitment to myself, and the results flow out of them.

So the way to always be a 10 in productivity is to choose one of these methods of operating and to move forward. The guiding question is: What will bring satisfaction? There is no absolute answer. It's a moving target. You have to monitor yourself as you go along and shift your strategy as appropriate. In all cases we need to affirm: What I am doing now is exactly what I need to be doing to be most productive—whether it is a results, action or time commitment. The absolute answers on how productive we should be in life are given in the book I mentioned earlier, *The Best Way*. You get to read it as soon as you pass from this world.

As a practical guide for being a "10" in productivity every day I suggest the following:

1. At the beginning of the day, decide what your priorities are and whether you want to make a results, action or time commitment to them.

2. Measure yourself at the end of the day on whether you kept your commitments and ask: Would I have done anything differently?

3. Periodically review the four questions with which I began this chapter.

4. Review what I said earlier about how to be a "10" every day in satisfaction.

AFFIRMATIONS

Measuring and Achieving Productivity

❖ I am totally productive.

❖ My productivity produces satisfaction.

CHAPTER 48

WHAT MAKES WORK FUN?: WHAT OTHERS SAY

In this book, I have discussed how you can move toward making your work and life a satisfying experience. Now, let's take a look at what others say makes this work fun. I gathered this data from a survey of over 200 professionals—including CPAs, lawyers, and engineers. The question I asked was, "What makes work fun for you?"

Before I give you their responses, I ask you to consider this question: What is it that makes work *not* fun for people? Your answer might be: problems at work, the people you have to deal with, hard projects, too many things to do, etc. What strikes me about the data I am going to give you is that the things which make work *not* fun for some are exactly what make work *fun* for others. In fact, if you look at the list below, the four examples I just gave are precisely the top four things that make work fun for people! This is evidence to me that whether your work is fun or not is totally up to you. Most of it doesn't have to do with the externals but with how you interpret and deal with them.

In the survey, I asked people to list the main thing that made work fun. Here are their answers in priority order:

1. Solving problems, working on challenges

2. The people I work with
3. A sense of accomplishment
4. Variety, new areas or things to work on
5. The work itself
6. Leading others
7. Independence

Let's briefly look at each of these.

1. SOLVING PROBLEMS, WORKING ON CHALLENGES

The largest number of people–28%–picked the ability to solve problems and work on challenges as the thing that made work most fun for them. This included the ability to be creative, to undertake large projects or to undertake new projects they haven't worked on before. It also included solving problems for clients or other people. Many of the responses included such words as "helping" or "serving" clients or "helping clients to succeed." Whether the aspect of "solving a problem" or the aspect of "helping others" predominates, solving problems and solving them for people are generally inextricable, and that's what makes work fun. So the very thing that makes work *not* fun for many— dealing with problems, hard challenges, people-problems—is what makes it fun for others.

2. THE PEOPLE I WORK WITH

The second thing that makes work fun, with 25% giving this response, is the people respondents work with. Words such as "rapport," "camaraderie" and "interaction" came up in describing what made work fun for people. Besides interaction with co-workers, responses also included interacting with clients or others.

Both types of response imply that it's not paper-work or project work that is most satisfying, but working with people themselves. A few of the responses described the atmosphere created by these people as "young, moving, creative, hard-working." Other listed solving problems *together* as what was most fun. The word "teamwork" combines response #1—meeting challenges or solving problems—and response #2—working together with people—into one focus. Other responses included getting positive feedback, having a good relationship with the boss and having good relationships with clients. I include these here because they focused not so much on the supervisory aspects of work but on the relationships themselves.

3. A SENSE OF ACCOMPLISHMENT

People spoke of a sense of accomplishment in two ways. One implied a sense of accomplishment from getting things done quantitatively, accomplishing a large number of things. The other was qualitative achievement; that is, reaching an objective or a goal, seeing results, seeing success. Some responses implied both: being efficient, being productive, completing things, doing a good job, doing things on time. One interesting description of accomplishment, used especially by lawyers, was the word "winning." Accomplishment is also related to response #1 as well.

4. VARIETY

People like a variety of tasks to work on or clients to work with. They like different jobs, the newness and the challenges that variety brings. Several people liked learning new fields or learning new skills in their work. So what makes work fun is the opposite of boredom.

These first four categories accounted for 84% of the responses. Most of the other responses were divided among the following:

5. THE WORK ITSELF

This means that people specifically like the technical aspect of their work. For instance, they liked working on a computer, or a legal file, or a specific engineering job.

6. LEADING OTHERS

Leading others is exemplified with words like, delegating well, assisting others, leading others, motivating others.

7. INDEPENDENCE

This is the ability to control your work. It implies being responsible to yourself, making money based on your own output, being in control of your future.

The number of things that make work fun for most people is not large. You can look at any item on this list with either fear or desire. I suggest desire. As I have been discussing throughout, it is your attitude that creates the reality, not external circumstances. If you're not having fun, how can you tell if you need to shift your attitude or not? First, if the circumstance is definitely undesirable, change it. If you can't change it, change jobs. If you choose not to change jobs, then change the thing from a "have to" to a "want to" —choose it, make it fun. If what you have is problems, make them fun. If you have to deal with people, make it fun. Does this sound familiar?

AFFIRMATIONS

Making Work Fun

❖ My work is fun.

❖ I have fun every day at work.

CHAPTER 49

CONCLUSION:
DON'T GO TO WORK UNLESS IT'S FUN!

I have a few concluding thoughts on the subject of not going to work unless it's fun. Actually, these thoughts are not really conclusive because this is an on-going inquiry for me. However, I need to end this book in one way or another, so let's pretend that this is the last word on the subject.

Initially, when reading the title you may have had the thought, "Oh, I may not be going to work any more!" After reading the book though, you should have the thought, "I *will* go to work and I look forward to it, because I always make my work fun."

In order to do this, we need to focus on work as part of the larger context—life! One of the wisest things I can say is what my wife periodically tells me, "Lighten up!" I love the idea of lightening up when it's applied to others. However, when applied to myself, it's a different story. Laughing at myself means I have to give up the grand images I have of myself or the illusions I maintain about the way reality should be. What it feels like before lightening up is: Universe – 1, Frank – 0. However, after permitting myself to laugh at myself, I soon realize the score is: Universe – 1, Frank – 1.

We both win! The Universe invariably wants to make me a winner. I just keep forgetting that *it* has to win in order for *me* to win. We are all in a win-win situation.

How to Create Satisfaction

In the motion picture *Oh, God,* with George Burns and John Denver, one of them, probably God, says: "God is a comedian playing to an audience with no sense of humor." There was a time in my life when I would have found that remark insulting. Now I think it's right on.

The parodox that applies to work as well as to life is: To take it seriously means to not take it so seriously. Remember, most of our funny memories and the stories we tell about them are based on personal "disasters," the things that went wrong. When work isn't fun, make it fun. When you can't seem to make work or life fun, have a good laugh!

1) THE NEW TIME MANAGEMENT WORKSHOP

ON AUDIO & VIDEO TAPE

This six-hour set of tapes is a live presentation of **The New Time Management Workshop** by Frank Sanitate. It is accompanied by a workbook to take you through a step-by-step process for mastering your use of time.

Is It Time?

It's time for you to become more:

● **Efficient** — Get more done in less time

● **Effective** — Work smarter instead of harder or longer

● **Satisfied** — Get more satisfaction from your work.

What You'll Learn

DRAINING THE SWAMP
1. **Self Analysis**
   - My Weaknesses
   - My Major Objective
   - Where My Time Goes
2. **One Way to Shift Your Attitude (and no longer have to say):**
   - "I have too many things to do and not enough time to do them."
   - "I hope I have the time to do this."
   - "I'm never finished."
3. **Seven Ways to Work on What Counts**
   - The Doing/Managing Ratio
   - Understanding Where Your Time Goes
   - Controlling Where Your Time Goes

4. Seven Ways to Delegate
- Overcoming Barriers to Delegating
- Utilizing Your Secretary
- Using Time-Saving Technology

5. One Way to Plan Your Life
- Working to Live Instead of Living to Work

FIGHTING THE ALLIGATORS

6. Four Ways to Plan and Set Priorities
- Setting and Sticking to Priorities
- Reducing Your Work Hours
- Long Range Planning
- How to Say "No" to Others
- How to Make Decisions

7. Six Ways to Stay in Control
- The Three Lists
- Daily Planning
- How to Not Let Anything Slip Through the Cracks

8. Six Ways to Eliminate Anxiety and Procrastination
- The Anatomy of Anxiety
- Why We Procrastinate
- Using Communication to Overcome Procrastination
- The Worst First Method

9. Three Ways to Control Interruptions
- Handling Walk-ins and Calls
- The Priority Hour

10. Four Ways to Manage the Phone
- Delegating the Phone
- 8 Steps to Getting Complete and Fewer Messages

11. Five Ways to Communicate Effectively
- Improving Communication with Your Staff or Boss
- The 8 Ingredients for Successful Meetings
- Coordinating Staff Activities

12. Seven Ways to Get and Stay Organized
- Orderly File Processing
- Clearing Up Your Piles
- Overcoming Indecision: The 3-Minute Rule
- Handling Paper and Mail

13. Five Ways to Create Time for Creativity and Well Being
- Creating Creative Time (The "Do What I Like" Day)
- Taking Vacations

What Others Say

● "I attribute the doubling of my income in my practice to attending Frank Sanitate's Time Management Workshop. I attend the workshop whenever I can as a refresher and always find it valuable." — Participant, Rockhill, SC

● "I am 100% more effective. This was the best seminar I ever attended. The practical tips are invaluable. Managing my time and prioritizing my work has made going to the office more enjoyable than before." — Participant, Raynham, MA

● "I've increased my effectiveness 85% and satisfaction 100%. The main thing I took away from the workshop is the knowledge that I can take control of my time both at work and otherwise, and ineffectiveness is not the result of external forces and demands." — Participant, Winnipeg, Manitoba

Extra Workbooks

Extra workbooks are available for both the audio and video programs. Have the whole office meet for a half-hour a week to use the tapes and participate in workbook exercises.

2) MASTERING TIME MANAGEMENT AND GOING BEYOND IT

A Six-Month Audio Tape Series
by Frank Sanitate

Time Management is a very simple matter: Do one thing at a time; do what's important; get help if you need it. That's the purpose of these audio-tapes: To support you in focusing on what's important to master your time, one month at a time, for the next six months.

What These Tapes Will Do For You

REMINDER/ANALYSIS - They will remind you to set new time management goals each month, to evaluate them and to analyze what went right and what went wrong.

ACTION - They will review and discuss key actions presented during the live workshop and new actions you can take to master time management.

ATTITUDE - They will help you to shift your thinking so that you can re-evaluate old attitudes, discard those that are not productive and take on new empowering attitudes.

Mastering Time Management:
Tape-A-Month Series

FEATURES

Tape 1

Attitude: • Time mastery means creating SATISFACTION in work and life
• Success comes from the 3 A's: Action, Attitude, Analysis

Action: • Daily and weekly planning
• Blocking out time

Tape 2

Attitude: • How to have all the time in the world
• Satisfaction: Having goals/ Giving up goals

Action: • Setting goals: Yearly, monthly
• Keeping track of things

Tape 3

Attitude: • The 4 stages of time: Boredom, scarcity, adequacy, abundance
• Creating an abundance of time
• Using vs. being used by technology

Action: • Creating daily satisfaction
• Managing the phone and fax
• The priority hour

Mastering Time Management:
Tape-A-Month Series

FEATURES

Tape 4

Attitude: • The 7 balances of life: End result vs. process, doing vs. managing, reoccuring daily activities vs. projects, billable vs. non-billable, work life vs. personal life, growth vs. coasting, availability vs. unavailability

Action • Going cold turkey
• Being verbal, truthful and tactful
• Create a balance by defining the balance

Tape 5

Attitude: • The 3 C's of satisfaction: Creation, Control, Completion
• The Quiz that will change your life

Action: • Clean it up: Your desk, your files, your office
• Goal-setting: Creating your life
• Mastering paper

Tape 6

Attitude: • Handling everything
• No more excess baggage
• The three levels of change

Action: • Cleaning up all of your anxieties
• Creating a path to ongoing development

INVESTMENT
• 30 Minutes per month
• $65—This breaks down to only $10.83 per month

HOW CAN YOU AFFORD NOT TO INVEST IN YOURSELF?

3) FRANK SANITATE ASSOCIATES SERVICES

Available from Frank Sanitate Associates are the following services:

1. IN-HOUSE WORKSHOPS

- Don't Go to Work Unless It's Fun: How to Become Happier and More Productive in Your Work

- The New Time Management Workshop

- The New Time Management Workshop for Secretaries and Assistants

- Stress or Satisfaction? How to Create a More Satisfying and Productive Worklife

- Problem-Solving and Creative Thinking for the 21st Century

- Management Excellence: How to Create a More Productive and Satisfying Workplace

- Communicating for Results: Speak Powerfully, Listen Productively

- How to Write Effectively

- Creating the Organization You Want: Increasing Productivity and Satisfaction

2. FACILITATING FIRM OR COMPANY RETREATS

We empower you to resolve problems, to plan, and to communicate at levels which will transform your organizations. Our two-day consulting workshop, **Creating the Organization You Want**, will enable you to achieve three goals:

1. To make a contribution

2. To make a profit

3. To have fun

3. BOOK—*THE $1\frac{1}{2}$MINUTE THEOLOGIAN*

Frank Sanitate is writing a book for "fallen-away" Christians and others who are seeking a philosophy which explains and celebrates their experience of the universe. If you want to receive information about it when it is published, please let us know.

ORDER FORM

Please Send Me:

1) THE NEW TIME MANAGEMENT WORKSHOP ON AUDIO & VIDEO TAPE!

___ Audio Cassette Programs @ $135.00 $ _____

___ Video Cassette Programs @ $235.00 $ _____

___ Extra Workshop Manuals @ $16.00 $ _____

2) MASTERING TIME MANAGEMENT & GOING BEYOND IT TAPE-A-MONTH SERIES

___ For Six Months @ $65.00 $ _____

3) ADDITIONAL COPIES OF *DON'T GO TO WORK UNLESS IT'S FUN!*

___ @ $14.95 each book $ _____

CA Residents Add 7.75% Tax $ _____

TOTAL $ _____

Payment:

Check Enclosed ___   VISA ___   MasterCard ___

Card # _____

Expiration Date _____

Signature _____

Name _____

Organization _____

Address _____

City _____ State _____

Zip _____ Telephone_____

4) PLEASE SEND ME INFORMATION ON FRANK SANITATE ASSOCIATES SERVICES

☐ In-House Workshops

☐ Facilitating Firm or Company Retreats

☐ Your next book—*The $1\frac{1}{2}$ Minute Theologian*

Make out your check and return this form to:

Frank Sanitate Associates

1152 Camino Manadero, Santa Barbara, CA 93111

(805) 967-7899 • FAX (805) 967-7303

ABOUT THE AUTHOR

Frank Sanitate was born in Detroit, Michigan, in 1941, the fifth of seven children of Italian immigrant parents. Graduating from Catholic University of America with a Bachelor's Degree in English Literature, he later received his MBA degree from Florida Atlantic University.

He taught English and Religion for five years at a Catholic high school in Buffalo, New York. During his college and teaching years, he was a member of the Christian Brothers, a Catholic religious order of teaching brothers. In 1970 he left the order and decided that teaching was not fun any longer. He then worked at The American Institute of CPAs administering continuing education seminars.

Realizing that it would be more fun to start his own business and teach seminars, he founded Frank Sanitate Associates in 1977. Since then he has taught tens of thousands of lawyers, CPAs and other professionals how to manage their time more effectively, how to communicate, how to think creatively and how to make their work more fun and more productive. Among his clients are General Electric, Hewlett Packard, MacDonald's, Greyhound and many other Fortune 500 companies. He is the best-known workshop instructor on time management for lawyers, CPAs and CAs in North America.

Even though he has always enjoyed his work, in 1989 he decided that on any given day he would not go to work unless it was fun. Since then he has either made it fun or he has not gone to work.

Frank Sanitate lives in Santa Barbara with his *wonderful* wife, Terry, and three *wonderful* children, James, Ian and Francesca. They are all usually fun.

NOTICE

Fifty percent of the net proceeds from sales of this book will be donated to ending global hunger and poverty. The money will be given to those groups and individuals doing the most to help the poorest to become self-sufficient.